50 Western Comfort Recipes for Home

By: Kelly Johnson

Table of Contents

- Beef Stroganoff
- Chicken Fried Steak
- Mashed Potatoes
- Biscuits and Gravy
- Meatloaf
- Chicken and Dumplings
- Roast Beef
- Macaroni and Cheese
- Cornbread
- Pot Roast
- Shepherd's Pie
- Enchiladas
- BBQ Ribs
- Fried Chicken
- Baked Beans
- Chili
- Sloppy Joes
- Stuffed Bell Peppers
- Beef Chili
- Pork Chops
- Salisbury Steak
- Baked Ziti
- Chicken Pot Pie
- Scalloped Potatoes
- Chicken Casserole
- Cowboy Beans
- Garlic Mashed Potatoes
- Southern Cornbread Dressing
- Green Bean Casserole
- Chicken Parmesan
- Pork Tenderloin
- Cheesy Grits
- Bacon-Wrapped Meatloaf
- Country Ham
- Fried Catfish
- Sweet Potato Casserole

- Potato Salad
- Buffalo Chicken Wings
- Tater Tot Casserole
- Beef and Noodle Casserole
- Lemon Bars
- Peach Cobbler
- Apple Pie
- Bread Pudding
- Chocolate Cake
- Banana Pudding
- Key Lime Pie
- Pecan Pie
- Rice Pudding
- Caramel Apple Cake

Beef Stroganoff

Ingredients:

- 1 pound beef sirloin or tenderloin, cut into thin strips
- 2 tablespoons olive oil or butter
- 1 large onion, finely chopped
- 2 cloves garlic, minced
- 8 ounces mushrooms, sliced (cremini or button)
- 1 cup beef broth
- 1 tablespoon Worcestershire sauce
- 1 tablespoon Dijon mustard
- 1 cup sour cream
- 1 tablespoon all-purpose flour (optional, for thickening)
- Salt and black pepper to taste
- 2 tablespoons fresh parsley, chopped (for garnish)
- Cooked egg noodles, rice, or mashed potatoes (for serving)

Instructions:

1. Cook the Beef:

1. **Heat Oil:** Heat the olive oil or butter in a large skillet over medium-high heat.
2. **Sear Beef:** Add the beef strips in a single layer. Cook for 2-3 minutes per side, or until browned but not fully cooked through. Remove the beef from the skillet and set aside.

2. Sauté Vegetables:

1. **Sauté Onions and Garlic:** In the same skillet, add the chopped onion and cook for 3-4 minutes until softened. Add the minced garlic and cook for another minute.
2. **Add Mushrooms:** Add the sliced mushrooms and cook until they are browned and tender, about 5 minutes.

3. Make the Sauce:

1. **Add Broth and Seasonings:** Stir in the beef broth, Worcestershire sauce, and Dijon mustard. Bring to a simmer and cook for 5 minutes, allowing the sauce to reduce slightly.
2. **Add Sour Cream:** Reduce heat to low and stir in the sour cream until well combined. If you prefer a thicker sauce, you can mix the flour with a little water to make a slurry and stir it into the sauce. Cook for another 2-3 minutes, until thickened.

4. Combine Beef and Sauce:

1. **Return Beef:** Return the browned beef to the skillet and stir to coat with the sauce. Cook for 2-3 minutes, or until the beef is cooked through and heated.

2. **Season:** Taste and adjust seasoning with salt and black pepper.

5. Serve:

1. **Garnish:** Garnish with chopped fresh parsley if desired.
2. **Serve:** Serve the beef stroganoff over cooked egg noodles, rice, or mashed potatoes.

Tips:

- **Beef:** For best results, use tender cuts of beef like sirloin or tenderloin. Avoid overcooking the beef to keep it tender.
- **Sour Cream:** Make sure to stir in the sour cream off the heat to prevent it from curdling.
- **Mushrooms:** You can use different types of mushrooms or add a splash of white wine for extra flavor.

Enjoy your delicious Beef Stroganoff, a classic comfort food that's perfect for a hearty meal!

Chicken Fried Steak

Ingredients:

For the Steaks:

- 4 beef cube steaks (about 1/2 inch thick)
- 1 cup all-purpose flour
- 1 teaspoon salt
- 1/2 teaspoon black pepper
- 1/2 teaspoon paprika
- 1/2 teaspoon garlic powder
- 2 large eggs
- 1 cup buttermilk
- 1 cup breadcrumbs (plain or seasoned)
- Vegetable oil (for frying)

For the Gravy:

- 1/4 cup all-purpose flour
- 2 cups milk
- 1 cup beef broth
- Salt and black pepper to taste

Instructions:

1. Prepare the Steaks:

1. **Pound the Steaks:** Place the cube steaks between two sheets of plastic wrap or parchment paper. Use a meat mallet to pound them to an even thickness, about 1/4 inch thick.
2. **Season Flour:** In a shallow dish, combine the flour, salt, pepper, paprika, and garlic powder.
3. **Prepare Breading:** In another shallow dish, whisk together the eggs and buttermilk. In a third shallow dish, place the breadcrumbs.

2. Bread the Steaks:

1. **Dredge in Flour:** Dredge each steak in the seasoned flour, coating both sides and shaking off any excess.
2. **Dip in Buttermilk:** Dip the floured steak into the buttermilk mixture, allowing excess to drip off.
3. **Coat with Breadcrumbs:** Coat the steak with breadcrumbs, pressing gently to adhere.

3. Fry the Steaks:

1. **Heat Oil:** In a large skillet, heat about 1/4 inch of vegetable oil over medium-high heat until hot.
2. **Fry Steaks:** Carefully add the breaded steaks to the hot oil. Fry for about 3-4 minutes per side, or until golden brown and crispy. Remove the steaks from the skillet and place them on a paper towel-lined plate to drain.

4. Make the Gravy:

1. **Remove Steaks:** Remove excess oil from the skillet, leaving about 2-3 tablespoons. Return the skillet to medium heat.
2. **Make Roux:** Sprinkle the flour into the hot oil and cook, stirring constantly, for 1-2 minutes to make a roux.
3. **Add Milk and Broth:** Gradually whisk in the milk and beef broth, scraping up any browned bits from the bottom of the skillet. Continue to cook and stir until the gravy thickens and is smooth.
4. **Season:** Season the gravy with salt and black pepper to taste.

5. Serve:

1. **Serve:** Spoon the gravy over the fried steaks. Serve with mashed potatoes, green beans, or your favorite sides.

Tips:

- **Steaks:** Cube steaks are commonly used for this recipe, but you can also use other cuts like round steak. Tenderize the meat if necessary.
- **Breading:** Ensure the oil is hot enough before frying to get a crispy coating. You may need to fry in batches.
- **Gravy:** Adjust the thickness of the gravy by adding more milk or broth if needed. If the gravy becomes too thick, add a little more liquid to reach your desired consistency.

Enjoy your classic Chicken Fried Steak with rich and creamy gravy!

Mashed Potatoes

Ingredients:

- 2 pounds russet potatoes (about 4 large potatoes)
- 1/2 cup milk (whole or 2%)
- 1/4 cup heavy cream (optional, for extra creaminess)
- 4 tablespoons butter (unsalted)
- Salt to taste
- Black pepper to taste
- 2-3 cloves garlic, minced (optional)
- Fresh chives or parsley, chopped (for garnish, optional)

Instructions:

1. Prepare the Potatoes:

1. **Peel and Cut:** Peel the potatoes and cut them into even chunks (about 1-2 inches). This helps them cook evenly.
2. **Rinse:** Rinse the potatoes under cold water to remove excess starch.

2. Cook the Potatoes:

1. **Boil:** Place the potatoes in a large pot and cover with cold water. Add a generous pinch of salt.
2. **Cook:** Bring to a boil over high heat. Reduce heat to medium and simmer until the potatoes are very tender, about 15-20 minutes. Test with a fork; the potatoes should easily break apart.

3. Mash the Potatoes:

1. **Drain:** Drain the potatoes well and return them to the pot or place in a large bowl.
2. **Mash:** Mash the potatoes using a potato masher, ricer, or food mill until smooth and free of lumps.

4. Add Dairy and Flavorings:

1. **Heat Dairy:** In a small saucepan, warm the milk and heavy cream over low heat. If you're using garlic, you can sauté it in a bit of butter until fragrant and then add it to the potatoes.
2. **Add Butter and Milk:** Stir the warm milk and cream mixture into the mashed potatoes, along with the butter. Continue to mix until the potatoes are creamy and smooth. Adjust the consistency with more milk or cream if needed.
3. **Season:** Season with salt and black pepper to taste.

5. Serve:

1. **Garnish:** Garnish with chopped fresh chives or parsley if desired.
2. **Serve Warm:** Serve immediately while warm.

Tips:

- **Texture:** For smoother potatoes, use a potato ricer or food mill. For a chunkier texture, use a masher.
- **Creaminess:** Adjust the amount of milk and cream to achieve your desired level of creaminess. Adding extra butter or cream can enhance richness.
- **Make Ahead:** You can make mashed potatoes ahead of time and reheat them gently over low heat, adding a bit more milk or cream if necessary to restore their texture.

Enjoy your creamy, comforting mashed potatoes as a perfect side dish for any meal!

Biscuits and Gravy

Ingredients:

For the Biscuits:

- 2 cups all-purpose flour
- 1 tablespoon baking powder
- 1/2 teaspoon baking soda
- 1/2 teaspoon salt
- 1/2 cup cold unsalted butter (1 stick), cut into small pieces
- 1 cup buttermilk (cold)

For the Sausage Gravy:

- 1 pound breakfast sausage (pork or turkey)
- 1/4 cup all-purpose flour
- 2 cups whole milk (or 2% for a lighter version)
- 1 cup chicken or beef broth
- Salt and black pepper to taste
- 1/4 teaspoon cayenne pepper (optional, for heat)

Instructions:

1. Make the Biscuits:

1. **Preheat Oven:** Preheat your oven to 425°F (220°C).
2. **Mix Dry Ingredients:** In a large bowl, whisk together the flour, baking powder, baking soda, and salt.
3. **Cut in Butter:** Add the cold butter to the flour mixture. Use a pastry cutter or your fingers to cut the butter into the flour until the mixture resembles coarse crumbs.
4. **Add Buttermilk:** Pour in the cold buttermilk and stir just until combined. The dough will be slightly sticky.
5. **Roll Out Dough:** Turn the dough out onto a floured surface and gently pat it to about 1-inch thickness.
6. **Cut Biscuits:** Use a floured biscuit cutter or a glass to cut out biscuits. Place them on a baking sheet, touching each other for soft sides.
7. **Bake:** Bake in the preheated oven for 12-15 minutes, or until the biscuits are golden brown.

2. Make the Sausage Gravy:

1. **Cook Sausage:** In a large skillet over medium heat, cook the sausage, breaking it up with a spoon, until browned and cooked through.

2. **Add Flour:** Sprinkle the flour over the cooked sausage and stir well to combine. Cook for 1-2 minutes to form a roux.
3. **Add Liquids:** Gradually whisk in the milk and broth, ensuring there are no lumps. Bring to a simmer and cook until the gravy thickens, about 5-7 minutes.
4. **Season:** Season with salt, black pepper, and cayenne pepper (if using). Adjust seasoning to taste.

3. Serve:

1. **Split Biscuits:** Split the baked biscuits in half.
2. **Top with Gravy:** Spoon the sausage gravy generously over the biscuit halves.

Tips:

- **Buttermilk:** For the best biscuits, make sure your buttermilk is cold and the butter is cold as well.
- **Consistency:** If the gravy is too thick, add more milk or broth. If it's too thin, let it simmer a bit longer or add a bit more flour.
- **Flavors:** For additional flavor, you can add a pinch of sage or thyme to the sausage gravy.

Enjoy your delicious Biscuits and Gravy as a hearty and comforting breakfast or brunch!

Meatloaf

Ingredients:

- 1 pound ground beef (80/20 blend for a good balance of meat and fat)
- 1/2 pound ground pork (optional, for added flavor and moisture)
- 1 large egg
- 1 cup breadcrumbs (plain or seasoned)
- 1/2 cup milk
- 1 small onion, finely chopped
- 2 cloves garlic, minced
- 1/4 cup ketchup
- 2 tablespoons Worcestershire sauce
- 1 teaspoon dried thyme
- 1 teaspoon dried oregano
- 1 teaspoon salt
- 1/2 teaspoon black pepper
- 1/2 cup shredded cheese (optional, for a cheesy meatloaf)
- 1/4 cup chopped fresh parsley (optional, for garnish)

For the Topping:

- 1/4 cup ketchup
- 2 tablespoons brown sugar
- 1 tablespoon Dijon mustard

Instructions:

1. Preheat Oven:

1. **Preheat:** Preheat your oven to 375°F (190°C).

2. Prepare the Meatloaf Mixture:

1. **Mix Ingredients:** In a large bowl, combine the ground beef, ground pork (if using), egg, breadcrumbs, milk, onion, garlic, ketchup, Worcestershire sauce, thyme, oregano, salt, and pepper. If adding cheese, mix it in at this stage.
2. **Combine:** Use your hands or a spoon to mix the ingredients until just combined. Avoid overmixing to keep the meatloaf tender.

3. Form the Meatloaf:

1. **Shape:** Transfer the meat mixture to a baking sheet or a loaf pan. Shape it into a loaf approximately 9x5 inches. If using a loaf pan, lightly grease it first.

4. Prepare the Topping:

1. **Mix Topping:** In a small bowl, mix together the ketchup, brown sugar, and Dijon mustard.
2. **Spread Topping:** Spread the topping mixture evenly over the top of the meatloaf.

5. Bake:

1. **Bake:** Bake in the preheated oven for 1 hour, or until the meatloaf is cooked through and has reached an internal temperature of 160°F (71°C). If using a loaf pan, it may take a bit longer.

6. Rest and Serve:

1. **Rest:** Let the meatloaf rest for about 10 minutes before slicing. This helps the juices redistribute and makes for easier slicing.
2. **Garnish:** Garnish with chopped parsley if desired.

Tips:

- **Ground Meat:** For a classic flavor, a combination of ground beef and pork works well, but you can use just ground beef if preferred.
- **Breadcrumbs:** If you don't have breadcrumbs, you can use crushed crackers or oats as a substitute.
- **Moisture:** To keep the meatloaf moist, avoid overmixing and don't skip the milk or egg.

Enjoy your delicious homemade meatloaf, a classic comfort food that pairs perfectly with mashed potatoes, green beans, or a simple salad!

Chicken and Dumplings

Ingredients:

For the Chicken:

- 1 whole chicken (about 3-4 pounds), cut into pieces, or 4 cups cooked, shredded chicken
- 1 onion, chopped
- 2 cloves garlic, minced
- 3 carrots, sliced
- 3 celery stalks, sliced
- 4 cups chicken broth
- 1 cup water
- 1 bay leaf
- 1 teaspoon dried thyme
- 1 teaspoon dried rosemary
- Salt and black pepper to taste

For the Dumplings:

- 2 cups all-purpose flour
- 2 teaspoons baking powder
- 1/2 teaspoon baking soda
- 1/2 teaspoon salt
- 1/4 cup cold unsalted butter (1/2 stick), cut into small pieces
- 1 cup buttermilk (or regular milk)

Instructions:

1. Cook the Chicken:

1. **Sauté Vegetables:** In a large pot or Dutch oven, heat a tablespoon of oil over medium heat. Add the chopped onion, garlic, carrots, and celery. Cook until the vegetables are softened, about 5 minutes.
2. **Add Chicken:** Add the chicken pieces (or shredded chicken if using pre-cooked) to the pot.
3. **Add Broth:** Pour in the chicken broth and water. Add the bay leaf, thyme, rosemary, salt, and black pepper.
4. **Simmer:** Bring to a boil, then reduce heat to low. Simmer for 30-40 minutes if using raw chicken, until the chicken is cooked through. If using pre-cooked chicken, simmer for about 15 minutes to allow flavors to meld.

2. Make the Dumplings:

1. **Combine Dry Ingredients:** In a large bowl, whisk together the flour, baking powder, baking soda, and salt.
2. **Cut in Butter:** Add the cold butter pieces to the flour mixture. Use a pastry cutter or your fingers to cut the butter into the flour until the mixture resembles coarse crumbs.
3. **Add Buttermilk:** Pour in the buttermilk and stir until just combined. The dough will be slightly lumpy.

3. Add Dumplings:

1. **Shred Chicken:** If using a whole chicken, remove it from the pot, shred the meat, and discard the bones. Return the shredded chicken to the pot.
2. **Add Dumplings:** Drop spoonfuls of the dumpling dough onto the simmering chicken mixture. They should be spaced apart as they will expand while cooking.
3. **Simmer:** Cover the pot with a lid and let the dumplings cook for 15-20 minutes, or until they are fluffy and cooked through. Do not lift the lid during this time.

4. Serve:

1. **Season:** Taste and adjust seasoning with additional salt and pepper if needed.
2. **Serve:** Ladle the chicken and dumplings into bowls and serve hot.

Tips:

- **Chicken:** You can use boneless, skinless chicken breasts or thighs for a quicker version, or a whole chicken for more flavor.
- **Dumplings:** For a lighter texture, avoid overmixing the dumpling dough. It's okay if the dough is a bit lumpy.
- **Thickness:** If you prefer a thicker stew, you can mix a tablespoon of flour or cornstarch with a little water and stir it into the simmering broth to thicken before adding the dumplings.

Enjoy your comforting Chicken and Dumplings, a classic dish that's perfect for a cozy meal!

Roast Beef

Ingredients:

- 3-4 pound beef roast (e.g., ribeye, sirloin, or chuck)
- 2 tablespoons olive oil
- Salt and black pepper to taste
- 4 cloves garlic, minced
- 2 tablespoons fresh rosemary, chopped (or 1 tablespoon dried rosemary)
- 2 tablespoons fresh thyme, chopped (or 1 tablespoon dried thyme)
- 1 onion, chopped
- 2 carrots, peeled and chopped
- 2 celery stalks, chopped
- 1 cup beef broth
- 1 cup red wine (optional, can substitute with more beef broth)
- 2 tablespoons all-purpose flour (optional, for thickening gravy)

Instructions:

1. Preheat Oven:

1. **Preheat:** Preheat your oven to 450°F (230°C).

2. Prepare the Roast:

1. **Season:** Pat the roast dry with paper towels. Rub all over with olive oil, then season generously with salt and black pepper. Rub the minced garlic, rosemary, and thyme into the roast.

3. Sear the Roast:

1. **Heat Skillet:** Heat a large ovenproof skillet or roasting pan over medium-high heat. Add a little olive oil if necessary.
2. **Sear Meat:** Sear the roast on all sides until browned, about 2-3 minutes per side. This step adds flavor and helps lock in juices.

4. Roast the Beef:

1. **Prepare Vegetables:** Place the chopped onion, carrots, and celery in the bottom of the roasting pan or around the roast in the skillet.
2. **Roast:** Place the seared roast on top of the vegetables in the pan. Transfer to the preheated oven and roast at 450°F (230°C) for 15 minutes.
3. **Reduce Heat:** Lower the oven temperature to 325°F (165°C) and continue roasting until the roast reaches your desired level of doneness. Use a meat thermometer for accuracy:
    - Rare: 125°F (52°C)

- Medium-Rare: 135°F (57°C)
- Medium: 145°F (63°C)
- Medium-Well: 150°F (66°C)
- Well-Done: 160°F (71°C)

4. **Rest:** Remove the roast from the oven and let it rest for 15-20 minutes before slicing. This allows the juices to redistribute.

5. Make the Gravy (Optional):

1. **Deglaze Pan:** Remove the roast from the pan and set aside. Place the pan over medium heat. Add the red wine (if using) and scrape up any browned bits from the bottom of the pan.
2. **Add Broth:** Stir in the beef broth and bring to a simmer. Let it cook for 5 minutes.
3. **Thicken Gravy:** If desired, mix the flour with a little water to make a slurry and stir it into the simmering broth to thicken. Cook for a few more minutes until thickened.

6. Serve:

1. **Slice:** Slice the roast beef against the grain into your preferred thickness.
2. **Serve:** Serve with the roasted vegetables and gravy.

Tips:

- **Resting Time:** Don't skip the resting period; it's crucial for juicy roast beef.
- **Vegetables:** The vegetables in the roasting pan will absorb flavors from the roast and can be served alongside or used to make gravy.
- **Gravy:** If you prefer a thicker gravy, increase the amount of flour or use a cornstarch slurry.

Enjoy your perfectly roasted beef, a classic and delicious centerpiece for any meal!

Macaroni and Cheese

Ingredients:

For the Macaroni:

- 2 cups elbow macaroni (or other pasta shape)
- Salt (for boiling pasta)

For the Cheese Sauce:

- 4 tablespoons unsalted butter
- 1/4 cup all-purpose flour
- 2 cups whole milk (or 2% for a lighter version)
- 1 cup heavy cream (optional, for extra creaminess)
- 2 cups shredded sharp cheddar cheese
- 1 cup shredded mozzarella cheese
- 1/2 cup grated Parmesan cheese
- 1 teaspoon Dijon mustard
- 1/2 teaspoon garlic powder
- 1/2 teaspoon onion powder
- 1/4 teaspoon paprika
- Salt and black pepper to taste

For the Topping (optional):

- 1/2 cup breadcrumbs (plain or seasoned)
- 2 tablespoons melted butter
- 1/4 cup grated Parmesan cheese

Instructions:

1. Cook the Macaroni:

1. **Boil Pasta:** Bring a large pot of salted water to a boil. Add the macaroni and cook according to the package instructions until al dente. Drain and set aside.

2. Make the Cheese Sauce:

1. **Melt Butter:** In a large saucepan, melt the butter over medium heat.
2. **Make Roux:** Stir in the flour and cook, stirring constantly, for about 1-2 minutes to make a roux. This will thicken the sauce.
3. **Add Milk and Cream:** Gradually whisk in the milk and heavy cream (if using). Continue to whisk to avoid lumps and cook until the mixture begins to thicken, about 5 minutes.

4. **Add Cheese:** Reduce heat to low and stir in the cheddar cheese, mozzarella cheese, and Parmesan cheese. Continue stirring until the cheese is fully melted and the sauce is smooth.
5. **Season:** Stir in the Dijon mustard, garlic powder, onion powder, paprika, salt, and black pepper. Adjust seasoning to taste.

3. Combine Pasta and Sauce:

1. **Mix Together:** Add the cooked macaroni to the cheese sauce and stir until the pasta is well coated with the sauce.

4. (Optional) Bake with Topping:

1. **Preheat Oven:** Preheat your oven to 375°F (190°C).
2. **Prepare Topping:** In a small bowl, mix the breadcrumbs with melted butter and grated Parmesan cheese.
3. **Transfer to Baking Dish:** Transfer the macaroni and cheese to a baking dish.
4. **Add Topping:** Sprinkle the breadcrumb mixture evenly over the top.
5. **Bake:** Bake in the preheated oven for 20-25 minutes, or until the topping is golden brown and the cheese is bubbly.

5. Serve:

1. **Enjoy:** Serve the macaroni and cheese hot, either straight from the pot or from the oven if baked.

Tips:

- **Cheese:** Use high-quality cheeses for the best flavor. Sharp cheddar adds a robust flavor, while mozzarella makes the sauce extra gooey.
- **Creaminess:** For extra creamy mac and cheese, use a combination of milk and heavy cream. If you prefer a lighter version, you can use milk alone.
- **Topping:** The breadcrumb topping adds a nice crunch, but the dish is also delicious without it.

Enjoy your homemade Macaroni and Cheese, a timeless comfort food that's always a hit!

Cornbread

Ingredients:

- 1 cup cornmeal
- 1 cup all-purpose flour
- 1/4 cup granulated sugar (adjust to taste)
- 1 tablespoon baking powder
- 1/2 teaspoon salt
- 1 cup buttermilk (or regular milk with 1 tablespoon lemon juice or vinegar)
- 2 large eggs
- 1/4 cup unsalted butter, melted
- 2 tablespoons butter (for greasing the pan)

Instructions:

1. Preheat Oven:

1. **Preheat Oven:** Preheat your oven to 425°F (220°C).

2. Prepare the Pan:

1. **Grease Pan:** Place the 2 tablespoons of butter in a 9-inch round or square baking pan. Put the pan in the preheated oven for about 5 minutes, or until the butter is melted and the pan is hot.

3. Mix Dry Ingredients:

1. **Combine Dry Ingredients:** In a large bowl, whisk together the cornmeal, flour, sugar, baking powder, and salt.

4. Mix Wet Ingredients:

1. **Combine Wet Ingredients:** In another bowl, whisk together the buttermilk, eggs, and melted butter.

5. Combine and Bake:

1. **Mix Together:** Pour the wet ingredients into the dry ingredients and stir until just combined. Do not overmix; it's okay if there are a few lumps.
2. **Pour Batter:** Carefully pour the batter into the hot, greased pan.
3. **Bake:** Bake in the preheated oven for 20-25 minutes, or until the cornbread is golden brown and a toothpick inserted into the center comes out clean.

6. Serve:

1. **Cool Slightly:** Let the cornbread cool in the pan for a few minutes before slicing.
2. **Enjoy:** Serve warm, optionally with butter or honey.

Tips:

- **Cornmeal:** Use coarse cornmeal for a more rustic texture or fine cornmeal for a smoother consistency.
- **Sweetness:** Adjust the amount of sugar based on your preference. Some people prefer a sweeter cornbread, while others like it less sweet.
- **Add-ins:** You can customize your cornbread by adding ingredients like shredded cheese, chopped jalapeños, or cooked bacon for extra flavor.

Enjoy your classic, homemade cornbread—a comforting and versatile addition to any meal!

Pot Roast

Ingredients:

- 3-4 pounds beef chuck roast (or another cut like brisket or round)
- 2 tablespoons olive oil
- Salt and black pepper to taste
- 1 large onion, chopped
- 3 cloves garlic, minced
- 4 carrots, peeled and cut into chunks
- 3 celery stalks, cut into chunks
- 1 pound baby potatoes or 4-5 large potatoes, peeled and cut into chunks
- 2 cups beef broth
- 1 cup red wine (optional, can substitute with more beef broth)
- 2 tablespoons tomato paste
- 2 tablespoons Worcestershire sauce
- 1 bay leaf
- 1 teaspoon dried thyme
- 1 teaspoon dried rosemary
- 1 tablespoon all-purpose flour (optional, for thickening gravy)

Instructions:

1. Preheat Oven:

1. **Preheat Oven:** Preheat your oven to 325°F (165°C).

2. Prepare the Roast:

1. **Season and Sear:** Pat the roast dry with paper towels. Season generously with salt and black pepper. Heat the olive oil in a large ovenproof pot or Dutch oven over medium-high heat. Sear the roast on all sides until browned, about 4-5 minutes per side. This step adds flavor and helps seal in the juices.

3. Add Vegetables and Aromatics:

1. **Sauté Vegetables:** Remove the roast from the pot and set aside. In the same pot, add the chopped onion and cook until softened, about 5 minutes. Add the minced garlic and cook for another minute.

4. Deglaze and Add Liquids:

1. **Add Tomato Paste:** Stir in the tomato paste and cook for 1-2 minutes.
2. **Deglaze:** Pour in the red wine (if using) and scrape up any browned bits from the bottom of the pot.

3. **Add Broth and Seasonings:** Stir in the beef broth, Worcestershire sauce, bay leaf, thyme, and rosemary.

5. Roast the Meat:

1. **Return Roast:** Place the seared roast back into the pot. Arrange the carrots, celery, and potatoes around the roast.
2. **Cover and Roast:** Cover the pot with a lid and transfer to the preheated oven. Roast for 3-4 hours, or until the meat is fork-tender and easily shreds.

6. Make the Gravy (Optional):

1. **Remove Meat and Vegetables:** Once the roast is done, remove the meat and vegetables from the pot and keep warm.
2. **Thicken Gravy:** If desired, make a slurry by mixing 1 tablespoon of flour with a little water and stir it into the simmering liquid in the pot. Cook for a few minutes until thickened.
3. **Adjust Seasoning:** Taste and adjust the seasoning with salt and pepper as needed.

7. Serve:

1. **Slice Meat:** Slice or shred the roast as desired.
2. **Serve:** Serve the roast with the vegetables and gravy on the side.

Tips:

- **Searing:** Don't skip the searing step, as it adds a depth of flavor to the roast.
- **Vegetables:** Feel free to add other vegetables like parsnips or turnips if you like.
- **Slow Cooker:** You can also make this recipe in a slow cooker. Follow the same steps for browning the meat and sautéing the vegetables, then transfer everything to a slow cooker and cook on low for 8-10 hours.

Enjoy your delicious, tender Pot Roast—a classic and satisfying meal that's perfect for family dinners!

Shepherd's Pie

Ingredients:

For the Meat Filling:

- 1 pound ground beef (or lamb for traditional Shepherd's Pie)
- 1 medium onion, chopped
- 2 cloves garlic, minced
- 2 carrots, peeled and diced
- 1 cup frozen peas
- 1 cup beef broth
- 1 tablespoon tomato paste
- 1 tablespoon Worcestershire sauce
- 1 teaspoon dried thyme
- 1 teaspoon dried rosemary
- Salt and black pepper to taste
- 2 tablespoons all-purpose flour (optional, for thickening)

For the Mashed Potatoes:

- 4 large potatoes, peeled and cubed
- 1/4 cup milk (more as needed)
- 1/4 cup unsalted butter
- Salt and black pepper to taste

Instructions:

1. Prepare the Mashed Potatoes:

1. **Cook Potatoes:** Place the cubed potatoes in a large pot and cover with cold water. Add a pinch of salt. Bring to a boil over high heat. Reduce heat and simmer until potatoes are tender, about 15-20 minutes.
2. **Drain and Mash:** Drain the potatoes and return them to the pot. Add the butter and milk. Mash until smooth and creamy. Season with salt and black pepper to taste. Set aside.

2. Prepare the Meat Filling:

1. **Cook Meat:** In a large skillet or saucepan, cook the ground beef over medium heat until browned. Drain excess fat if necessary.
2. **Sauté Vegetables:** Add the chopped onion, garlic, and carrots to the skillet. Cook until the vegetables are softened, about 5 minutes.
3. **Add Peas and Seasonings:** Stir in the frozen peas, tomato paste, Worcestershire sauce, thyme, rosemary, salt, and black pepper. Cook for 1-2 minutes.

4. **Add Broth:** Pour in the beef broth. Bring to a simmer and cook for 5-7 minutes, until the mixture has thickened. If needed, stir in the flour to thicken the mixture further. Taste and adjust seasoning.

3. Assemble and Bake:

1. **Preheat Oven:** Preheat your oven to 400°F (200°C).
2. **Transfer Meat Mixture:** Transfer the meat filling to a baking dish (about 9x9 inches or equivalent).
3. **Top with Mashed Potatoes:** Spread the mashed potatoes evenly over the meat filling. Use a fork to create a textured surface on the potatoes if desired.
4. **Bake:** Bake in the preheated oven for 20-25 minutes, or until the top is golden brown and the filling is bubbling.

4. Serve:

1. **Cool Slightly:** Let the Shepherd's Pie cool for a few minutes before serving.
2. **Enjoy:** Serve warm.

Tips:

- **Ground Meat:** Traditional Shepherd's Pie uses ground lamb, but ground beef is a common substitute.
- **Mashed Potatoes:** For extra creaminess, you can mix in a bit of sour cream or cream cheese into the mashed potatoes.
- **Vegetables:** You can add other vegetables like corn or mushrooms to the meat filling for added flavor.

Enjoy your delicious Shepherd's Pie—a hearty and satisfying meal perfect for any day of the week!

Enchiladas

Ingredients:

For the Filling:

- 1 pound ground beef or shredded chicken (cooked)
- 1 medium onion, finely chopped
- 2 cloves garlic, minced
- 1 cup shredded cheese (cheddar, Monterey Jack, or a blend)
- 1 can (14.5 oz) diced tomatoes (optional, for a more flavorful filling)
- 1 tablespoon chili powder
- 1 teaspoon ground cumin
- 1/2 teaspoon paprika
- Salt and black pepper to taste
- 1/4 cup chopped fresh cilantro (optional)

For the Enchilada Sauce:

- 2 tablespoons vegetable oil
- 2 tablespoons all-purpose flour
- 1/4 cup chili powder
- 1/2 teaspoon ground cumin
- 1/2 teaspoon garlic powder
- 1/2 teaspoon onion powder
- 1/4 teaspoon salt
- 2 cups chicken or beef broth
- 1 can (8 oz) tomato sauce

For Assembly:

- 10-12 corn or flour tortillas (6-inch or 8-inch)
- 2 cups shredded cheese (cheddar, Monterey Jack, or a blend)
- Fresh cilantro for garnish (optional)

Instructions:

1. Prepare the Enchilada Sauce:

1. **Heat Oil:** In a medium saucepan, heat the vegetable oil over medium heat.
2. **Make Roux:** Stir in the flour and cook for 1-2 minutes until lightly browned.
3. **Add Spices:** Add the chili powder, cumin, garlic powder, onion powder, and salt. Stir to combine and cook for an additional 30 seconds.

4. **Add Liquids:** Gradually whisk in the broth and tomato sauce. Continue to whisk until smooth. Bring to a simmer and cook for about 10 minutes, until the sauce has thickened. Set aside.

2. Prepare the Filling:

1. **Cook Meat:** In a large skillet, cook the ground beef over medium heat until browned. Drain any excess fat.
2. **Add Vegetables:** Add the chopped onion and garlic to the skillet and cook until softened, about 5 minutes.
3. **Season:** Stir in the chili powder, cumin, paprika, salt, and black pepper. If using diced tomatoes, add them now.
4. **Combine:** Mix in the shredded cheese and cilantro (if using) until well combined. Remove from heat.

3. Assemble the Enchiladas:

1. **Preheat Oven:** Preheat your oven to 375°F (190°C).
2. **Warm Tortillas:** If using corn tortillas, heat them in a dry skillet or wrap them in foil and warm in the oven to make them more pliable.
3. **Fill Tortillas:** Spread a small amount of enchilada sauce in the bottom of a baking dish. Spoon about 2-3 tablespoons of the meat mixture down the center of each tortilla. Roll up the tortillas and place them seam-side down in the baking dish.
4. **Add Sauce and Cheese:** Pour the remaining enchilada sauce over the top of the rolled tortillas. Sprinkle the additional shredded cheese evenly over the top.

4. Bake:

1. **Bake:** Bake in the preheated oven for 20-25 minutes, or until the cheese is melted and bubbly and the sauce is hot.

5. Serve:

1. **Garnish:** Garnish with fresh cilantro if desired.
2. **Enjoy:** Serve hot with your favorite toppings such as sour cream, salsa, or guacamole.

Tips:

- **Tortillas:** Corn tortillas are traditional for enchiladas, but flour tortillas can be used if preferred.
- **Sauce:** Adjust the level of spiciness in the enchilada sauce by adding more or less chili powder.
- **Make-Ahead:** Enchiladas can be assembled ahead of time and refrigerated for up to 24 hours before baking.

Enjoy your homemade enchiladas—a delicious and satisfying meal that's always a crowd-pleaser!

BBQ Ribs

Ingredients:

For the Ribs:

- 2 racks of pork baby back ribs (about 2-3 pounds each)
- 1 tablespoon olive oil
- Salt and black pepper to taste

For the Dry Rub:

- 2 tablespoons brown sugar
- 1 tablespoon paprika
- 1 tablespoon chili powder
- 1 teaspoon garlic powder
- 1 teaspoon onion powder
- 1 teaspoon ground cumin
- 1/2 teaspoon cayenne pepper (optional, for heat)
- 1/2 teaspoon dried oregano
- 1/2 teaspoon dried thyme
- 1/2 teaspoon salt
- 1/2 teaspoon black pepper

For the BBQ Sauce:

- 1 cup ketchup
- 1/2 cup apple cider vinegar
- 1/4 cup brown sugar
- 1/4 cup honey
- 1 tablespoon Worcestershire sauce
- 1 tablespoon soy sauce
- 1 tablespoon Dijon mustard
- 1 teaspoon smoked paprika
- 1/2 teaspoon garlic powder
- 1/2 teaspoon onion powder
- Salt and black pepper to taste

Instructions:

1. Prepare the Ribs:

1. **Remove Membrane:** If necessary, remove the thin membrane from the back of the ribs. This can be done by loosening it with a knife and pulling it off with your fingers or a paper towel.

2. **Season Ribs:** Rub the ribs with olive oil, then season generously with salt and black pepper.

2. Apply the Dry Rub:

1. **Mix Dry Rub:** In a small bowl, combine the brown sugar, paprika, chili powder, garlic powder, onion powder, cumin, cayenne pepper (if using), oregano, thyme, salt, and black pepper.
2. **Apply Rub:** Rub the dry rub mixture evenly over both sides of the ribs. Let the ribs sit for at least 30 minutes, or refrigerate for several hours or overnight for more flavor.

3. Make the BBQ Sauce:

1. **Combine Ingredients:** In a medium saucepan, combine all the BBQ sauce ingredients: ketchup, apple cider vinegar, brown sugar, honey, Worcestershire sauce, soy sauce, Dijon mustard, smoked paprika, garlic powder, onion powder, salt, and black pepper.
2. **Simmer:** Bring the sauce to a simmer over medium heat, stirring occasionally. Cook for 10-15 minutes, or until slightly thickened. Remove from heat and set aside.

4. Cook the Ribs:

Oven Method (Low and Slow):

1. **Preheat Oven:** Preheat your oven to 275°F (135°C).
2. **Wrap Ribs:** Place the ribs on a large piece of aluminum foil, bone-side down. Wrap tightly to create a sealed packet. Place the wrapped ribs on a baking sheet.
3. **Bake:** Bake in the preheated oven for 2.5 to 3 hours, or until the ribs are tender and the meat pulls away from the bones easily.

Grill Method (Finish on the Grill):

1. **Preheat Grill:** Preheat your grill to medium heat.
2. **Grill Ribs:** Remove the ribs from the oven and discard the foil. Brush the ribs with the BBQ sauce.
3. **Grill:** Place the ribs on the grill and cook over indirect heat for about 10-15 minutes, turning and basting with additional BBQ sauce, until caramelized and slightly crispy on the edges.

5. Serve:

1. **Rest:** Let the ribs rest for a few minutes before cutting.
2. **Slice and Serve:** Cut between the bones to separate the ribs. Serve with extra BBQ sauce on the side.

Tips:

- **Slow Cooking:** For even more tender ribs, you can cook them at a lower temperature for a longer period.
- **BBQ Sauce:** Feel free to adjust the BBQ sauce ingredients to suit your taste or use your favorite store-bought sauce.
- **Grilling:** If you prefer, you can cook the ribs entirely on the grill using a low and slow method for about 4-5 hours.

Enjoy your homemade BBQ Ribs, a delicious and satisfying dish perfect for summer gatherings or any time you crave smoky, tender meat!

Fried Chicken

Ingredients:

For the Chicken:

- 3-4 pounds chicken pieces (legs, thighs, wings, or breasts), bone-in and skin-on

For the Brine (Optional but recommended):

- 4 cups buttermilk (or milk with 1 tablespoon lemon juice or vinegar)
- 2 tablespoons salt
- 1 tablespoon sugar

For the Flour Coating:

- 2 cups all-purpose flour
- 1 tablespoon paprika
- 1 tablespoon garlic powder
- 1 tablespoon onion powder
- 1 teaspoon dried thyme
- 1 teaspoon dried oregano
- 1 teaspoon cayenne pepper (optional, for heat)
- 1 teaspoon salt
- 1 teaspoon black pepper

For Frying:

- 2-3 cups vegetable oil (or enough to fill your skillet 1-2 inches deep)

Instructions:

1. Brine the Chicken (Optional):

1. **Prepare Brine:** In a large bowl, whisk together the buttermilk, salt, and sugar.
2. **Brine Chicken:** Submerge the chicken pieces in the buttermilk mixture. Cover and refrigerate for at least 2 hours, or overnight for best results.

2. Prepare the Flour Coating:

1. **Mix Flour Coating:** In a large bowl, combine the flour, paprika, garlic powder, onion powder, thyme, oregano, cayenne pepper, salt, and black pepper.

3. Dredge the Chicken:

1. **Remove Chicken from Brine:** If brined, remove the chicken from the buttermilk and let any excess drip off.
2. **Coat Chicken:** Dredge each piece of chicken in the seasoned flour mixture, pressing lightly to ensure the flour sticks. Shake off excess flour.

4. Fry the Chicken:

1. **Heat Oil:** In a large, heavy skillet or Dutch oven, heat the vegetable oil over medium-high heat until it reaches 350°F (175°C). Use a thermometer to check the temperature.
2. **Fry Chicken:** Carefully add a few pieces of chicken to the hot oil, making sure not to overcrowd the pan. Fry the chicken for 8-10 minutes per side, or until the internal temperature reaches 165°F (74°C) and the coating is golden brown and crispy. Adjust the heat as necessary to maintain the oil temperature.
3. **Drain:** Transfer the fried chicken to a wire rack set over a baking sheet to drain excess oil. Alternatively, you can place the chicken on paper towels.

5. Serve:

1. **Cool Slightly:** Let the chicken cool slightly before serving. This helps the coating to stay crispy.
2. **Enjoy:** Serve hot with your favorite sides.

Tips:

- **Oil Temperature:** Maintaining the proper oil temperature is key to achieving a crispy coating. If the oil is too hot, the coating may burn before the chicken is cooked through. If it's too cool, the coating can become greasy.
- **Resting:** Allowing the chicken to rest after frying helps the coating to set and become even crispier.
- **Flavored Flour:** For added flavor, you can mix in some grated Parmesan cheese or additional spices into the flour coating.

Enjoy your homemade Fried Chicken—a delicious and classic comfort food that's always a crowd-pleaser!

Baked Beans

Ingredients:

For the Beans:

- 4 cups dried navy beans (or other small white beans)
- 1/2 pound bacon, chopped
- 1 medium onion, finely chopped
- 2 cloves garlic, minced
- 1/2 cup brown sugar
- 1/4 cup molasses
- 1/4 cup ketchup
- 2 tablespoons Dijon mustard
- 2 tablespoons Worcestershire sauce
- 1 teaspoon smoked paprika (or regular paprika)
- 1/2 teaspoon black pepper
- 1/2 teaspoon salt
- 2 cups water (or more as needed)

Instructions:

1. Prepare the Beans:

1. **Soak Beans:** Place the dried beans in a large bowl and cover with water. Soak overnight, or for at least 8 hours. Alternatively, for a quicker method, bring the beans and water to a boil for 2 minutes, then remove from heat and let them sit, covered, for 1 hour.
2. **Drain and Rinse:** Drain and rinse the beans after soaking.

2. Preheat Oven:

1. **Preheat Oven:** Preheat your oven to 325°F (165°C).

3. Cook the Bacon:

1. **Cook Bacon:** In a large skillet or Dutch oven, cook the chopped bacon over medium heat until crispy. Remove the bacon with a slotted spoon and set aside, leaving the bacon fat in the pan.

4. Prepare the Beans Mixture:

1. **Sauté Onions and Garlic:** In the same skillet with bacon fat, add the chopped onion and cook until softened, about 5 minutes. Add the minced garlic and cook for an additional minute.
2. **Combine Ingredients:** In the skillet with the onions and garlic, stir in the brown sugar, molasses, ketchup, Dijon mustard, Worcestershire sauce, smoked paprika, black

pepper, and salt. Cook for a few minutes until the mixture is well combined and heated through.

5. Combine and Bake:

1. **Mix Beans:** In a large ovenproof dish or Dutch oven, combine the soaked beans, bacon, and the sauce mixture.
2. **Add Water:** Add 2 cups of water to the beans. Stir to combine.
3. **Bake:** Cover the dish with a lid or aluminum foil and bake in the preheated oven for 2.5 to 3 hours, or until the beans are tender. Check occasionally, and add more water if necessary to keep the beans covered with liquid.

6. Serve:

1. **Cool Slightly:** Allow the beans to cool slightly before serving. They will thicken as they cool.
2. **Enjoy:** Serve warm as a delicious side dish.

Tips:

- **Beans:** If using canned beans, skip the soaking step and reduce the baking time. You can use about 4 cans of drained and rinsed beans.
- **Thickness:** If you prefer a thicker sauce, you can cook the beans uncovered during the last 30 minutes of baking.
- **Flavor Variations:** Add a bit of chopped bell pepper, jalapeño, or a splash of vinegar for additional flavor if desired.

Enjoy your homemade Baked Beans—a classic and comforting dish that's sure to be a hit at any gathering!

Chili

Ingredients:

- **2 tablespoons vegetable oil**
- **1 pound ground beef**
- **1 large onion, chopped**
- **2 cloves garlic, minced**
- **1 bell pepper, chopped** (any color)
- **2 (15-ounce) cans diced tomatoes** (with juice)
- **1 (15-ounce) can tomato sauce**
- **1 (15-ounce) can kidney beans**, drained and rinsed
- **1 (15-ounce) can black beans**, drained and rinsed
- **2 tablespoons chili powder**
- **1 tablespoon ground cumin**
- **1 teaspoon paprika**
- **1/2 teaspoon dried oregano**
- **1/2 teaspoon cayenne pepper** (optional, for heat)
- **Salt and black pepper to taste**
- **1 cup beef broth** (or water)
- **1 tablespoon Worcestershire sauce**
- **1 tablespoon sugar** (optional, to balance acidity)
- **1 cup shredded cheese** (cheddar or Monterey Jack, optional, for topping)
- **Sour cream** (optional, for topping)
- **Chopped green onions** (optional, for topping)
- **Fresh cilantro** (optional, for garnish)

Instructions:

1. Cook the Beef:

1. **Heat Oil:** In a large pot or Dutch oven, heat the vegetable oil over medium-high heat.
2. **Brown Beef:** Add the ground beef and cook, breaking it apart with a spoon, until browned and cooked through. Drain any excess fat.

2. Add Vegetables:

1. **Sauté Vegetables:** Add the chopped onion, garlic, and bell pepper to the pot. Cook until the vegetables are softened, about 5 minutes.

3. Add Spices and Liquids:

1. **Add Spices:** Stir in the chili powder, cumin, paprika, oregano, cayenne pepper (if using), salt, and black pepper. Cook for 1-2 minutes to toast the spices.
2. **Add Tomatoes and Beans:** Add the diced tomatoes, tomato sauce, kidney beans, black beans, beef broth, Worcestershire sauce, and sugar (if using). Stir well to combine.

4. Simmer:

1. **Simmer Chili:** Bring the chili to a boil, then reduce heat to low. Simmer uncovered for 30-45 minutes, stirring occasionally, until the chili is thickened and the flavors are well combined. Adjust seasoning if needed.

5. Serve:

1. **Top and Garnish:** Serve the chili hot, topped with shredded cheese, sour cream, chopped green onions, and fresh cilantro if desired.

Tips:

- **Texture:** For a thicker chili, simmer it uncovered for a longer time. You can also mash some of the beans to thicken it.
- **Beans:** Feel free to use other types of beans or a mix of beans according to your preference.
- **Heat Level:** Adjust the level of heat by adding more or less cayenne pepper or including a chopped jalapeño pepper with the onions and garlic.

Enjoy your homemade chili—a warm, satisfying dish perfect for cooler weather or any time you crave comfort food!

Sloppy Joes

Ingredients:

- **1 pound ground beef** (or ground turkey for a lighter option)
- **1 medium onion, finely chopped**
- **1 bell pepper, finely chopped** (any color)
- **2 cloves garlic, minced**
- **1 cup ketchup**
- **1/4 cup tomato paste**
- **2 tablespoons Worcestershire sauce**
- **2 tablespoons brown sugar**
- **1 tablespoon yellow mustard**
- **1 teaspoon paprika**
- **1/2 teaspoon garlic powder**
- **1/2 teaspoon onion powder**
- **Salt and black pepper to taste**
- **1/2 cup water** (or beef broth for more flavor)
- **4-6 hamburger buns**, toasted if desired

Instructions:

1. Cook the Beef:

1. **Brown Beef:** In a large skillet or sauté pan, cook the ground beef over medium heat until browned. Break it apart with a spoon as it cooks. Drain any excess fat.

2. Add Vegetables:

1. **Sauté Vegetables:** Add the chopped onion, bell pepper, and minced garlic to the skillet. Cook until the vegetables are softened, about 5 minutes.

3. Add Sauce Ingredients:

1. **Combine Sauces:** Stir in the ketchup, tomato paste, Worcestershire sauce, brown sugar, mustard, paprika, garlic powder, and onion powder. Mix well.
2. **Add Water/Broth:** Pour in the water or beef broth. Stir to combine and let the mixture come to a simmer.

4. Simmer:

1. **Simmer Mixture:** Reduce the heat to low and let the mixture simmer uncovered for 15-20 minutes, or until it thickens and the flavors meld. Stir occasionally. Adjust seasoning with salt and pepper to taste.

5. Serve:

1. **Assemble Sandwiches:** Spoon the sloppy joe mixture onto the bottom half of the hamburger buns. Top with the other half of the bun.
2. **Optional:** You can add toppings like pickles, onions, or shredded cheese if desired.

Tips:

- **Consistency:** If the mixture is too thick, add a bit more water or broth. If it's too thin, let it simmer longer to reduce and thicken.
- **Make Ahead:** Sloppy Joe mixture can be made ahead of time and stored in the refrigerator for up to 3 days. Reheat before serving.
- **Variations:** For a twist, you can add a splash of hot sauce for heat or a tablespoon of BBQ sauce for a smoky flavor.

Enjoy your homemade Sloppy Joes—a classic and satisfying comfort food that's perfect for a casual meal!

Stuffed Bell Peppers

Ingredients:

- **4 large bell peppers** (any color)
- **1 pound ground beef** (or ground turkey or chicken)
- **1 cup cooked rice** (white or brown)
- **1 can (15 ounces) diced tomatoes**, drained
- **1/2 cup onion**, finely chopped
- **2 cloves garlic**, minced
- **1 cup shredded cheese** (cheddar, mozzarella, or a blend)
- **1 egg**, beaten
- **2 tablespoons tomato paste**
- **1 tablespoon Worcestershire sauce**
- **1 teaspoon dried oregano**
- **1 teaspoon dried basil**
- **Salt and black pepper to taste**
- **2 tablespoons olive oil** (optional, for drizzling)

Instructions:

1. Prepare the Peppers:

1. **Preheat Oven:** Preheat your oven to 375°F (190°C).
2. **Prepare Peppers:** Cut the tops off the bell peppers and remove the seeds and membranes. If needed, trim the bottoms slightly to make sure they stand upright.

2. Cook the Filling:

1. **Brown Meat:** In a large skillet, heat a bit of olive oil over medium heat. Add the ground beef (or other meat) and cook until browned. Drain any excess fat.
2. **Add Vegetables:** Add the chopped onion and garlic to the skillet. Cook until the onion is translucent and the garlic is fragrant, about 5 minutes.
3. **Combine Ingredients:** Stir in the cooked rice, drained diced tomatoes, tomato paste, Worcestershire sauce, oregano, basil, and beaten egg. Mix well and cook for a few more minutes to combine the flavors. Season with salt and black pepper to taste.
4. **Add Cheese:** Stir in 1/2 cup of the shredded cheese, allowing it to melt into the mixture.

3. Stuff the Peppers:

1. **Fill Peppers:** Spoon the meat and rice mixture into each bell pepper, packing it in firmly.
2. **Top with Cheese:** Place the stuffed peppers upright in a baking dish. Sprinkle the remaining shredded cheese over the tops of the stuffed peppers.

4. Bake:

1. **Bake Peppers:** Drizzle the peppers with a little olive oil if desired. Cover the baking dish with aluminum foil and bake in the preheated oven for 30 minutes.
2. **Uncover and Continue Baking:** Remove the foil and bake for an additional 10-15 minutes, or until the peppers are tender and the cheese is melted and bubbly.

5. Serve:

1. **Cool Slightly:** Allow the peppers to cool for a few minutes before serving.
2. **Enjoy:** Serve warm with your favorite sides or as a main dish.

Tips:

- **Peppers:** If you prefer, you can also use smaller peppers or different colors for variety. Just adjust the baking time as needed.
- **Rice:** Substitute the rice with quinoa or couscous for a different twist.
- **Vegetarian Option:** For a vegetarian version, you can use black beans, corn, and cheese as the filling, omitting the meat.

Enjoy your Stuffed Bell Peppers—a colorful, tasty, and satisfying dish that's perfect for a wholesome meal!

Beef Chili

Ingredients:

- **1 pound ground beef** (or ground chuck for more flavor)
- **1 medium onion, chopped**
- **2 cloves garlic, minced**
- **1 bell pepper, chopped** (any color)
- **1 can (15 ounces) diced tomatoes** (with juice)
- **1 can (15 ounces) tomato sauce**
- **1 can (15 ounces) kidney beans**, drained and rinsed
- **1 can (15 ounces) black beans**, drained and rinsed
- **2 tablespoons chili powder**
- **1 tablespoon ground cumin**
- **1 teaspoon paprika**
- **1/2 teaspoon dried oregano**
- **1/2 teaspoon cayenne pepper** (optional, for heat)
- **Salt and black pepper to taste**
- **1 cup beef broth** (or water)
- **1 tablespoon Worcestershire sauce**
- **1 tablespoon sugar** (optional, to balance acidity)
- **1 cup shredded cheese** (cheddar or Monterey Jack, optional, for topping)
- **Sour cream** (optional, for topping)
- **Chopped green onions** (optional, for topping)
- **Fresh cilantro** (optional, for garnish)

Instructions:

1. Cook the Beef:

1. **Brown Beef:** In a large pot or Dutch oven, heat a little oil over medium heat. Add the ground beef and cook, breaking it apart with a spoon, until browned. Drain any excess fat.

2. Add Vegetables:

1. **Sauté Vegetables:** Add the chopped onion, bell pepper, and minced garlic to the pot. Cook until the vegetables are softened, about 5 minutes.

3. Add Spices and Liquids:

1. **Add Spices:** Stir in the chili powder, cumin, paprika, oregano, cayenne pepper (if using), salt, and black pepper. Cook for 1-2 minutes to toast the spices.
2. **Add Tomatoes and Beans:** Stir in the diced tomatoes, tomato sauce, kidney beans, black beans, beef broth, Worcestershire sauce, and sugar (if using). Mix well.

4. Simmer:

1. **Simmer Chili:** Bring the chili to a boil, then reduce the heat to low. Simmer uncovered for 30-45 minutes, or until the chili is thickened and the flavors are well combined. Stir occasionally. Adjust seasoning as needed.

5. Serve:

1. **Top and Garnish:** Serve the chili hot, topped with shredded cheese, sour cream, chopped green onions, and fresh cilantro if desired.

Tips:

- **Thickness:** For a thicker chili, let it simmer uncovered for a longer period or mash some of the beans.
- **Heat Level:** Adjust the heat level by adding more or less cayenne pepper or including a chopped jalapeño pepper with the onions and garlic.
- **Make Ahead:** Chili can be made ahead of time and stored in the refrigerator for up to 3 days or frozen for up to 3 months. Reheat thoroughly before serving.

Enjoy your homemade Beef Chili—a rich, satisfying dish that's perfect for cooler weather or any time you crave a hearty meal!

Pork Chops

Ingredients:

- **4 bone-in pork chops** (about 1-inch thick)
- **2 tablespoons olive oil**
- **Salt and black pepper to taste**
- **1 teaspoon garlic powder**
- **1 teaspoon onion powder**
- **1 teaspoon paprika**
- **1/2 teaspoon dried thyme**
- **1/2 teaspoon dried rosemary**
- **1/2 teaspoon dried oregano**
- **1/2 cup chicken broth** (or water)
- **1 tablespoon butter** (optional, for extra richness)

Instructions:

1. Prepare the Pork Chops:

1. **Preheat Oven (if baking):** Preheat your oven to 375°F (190°C) if you plan to bake the pork chops.
2. **Season Pork Chops:** Pat the pork chops dry with paper towels. Season both sides generously with salt and black pepper. Rub the garlic powder, onion powder, paprika, thyme, rosemary, and oregano on both sides.

2. Cook the Pork Chops:

Pan-Frying Method:

1. **Heat Oil:** In a large skillet, heat the olive oil over medium-high heat.
2. **Sear Pork Chops:** Add the pork chops to the skillet. Cook for 4-5 minutes on each side, or until the chops are browned and have an internal temperature of 145°F (63°C). Remove the chops from the skillet and set aside.
3. **Deglaze Skillet (optional):** Add a splash of chicken broth to the skillet to deglaze, scraping up any browned bits from the bottom of the pan. Pour this over the pork chops before serving.

Baking Method:

1. **Sear Pork Chops:** In a skillet, heat olive oil over medium-high heat. Sear the pork chops for 2-3 minutes per side, until browned.
2. **Bake:** Transfer the seared pork chops to a baking dish. Pour the chicken broth around the chops. Bake in the preheated oven for 15-20 minutes, or until the internal temperature reaches 145°F (63°C).

3. **Rest and Serve:** Let the pork chops rest for 5 minutes before serving. Optionally, you can melt butter in the pan and pour it over the chops before serving.

Grilling Method:

1. **Preheat Grill:** Preheat your grill to medium-high heat.
2. **Grill Pork Chops:** Grill the pork chops for 4-5 minutes per side, or until the internal temperature reaches 145°F (63°C). Be sure to check for doneness with a meat thermometer.

3. Serve:

1. **Rest and Slice:** Let the pork chops rest for a few minutes before slicing. This helps the juices redistribute.
2. **Enjoy:** Serve with your favorite sides like mashed potatoes, vegetables, or a fresh salad.

Tips:

- **Tenderizing:** For extra tenderness, you can brine the pork chops in a solution of water, salt, and sugar for a few hours before cooking.
- **Flavor Variations:** Try different seasonings or marinades for varied flavors. For a sweet touch, you can use a honey glaze or apple sauce.

Enjoy your perfectly cooked Pork Chops—a versatile and delicious option for any meal!

Salisbury Steak

Ingredients:

For the Salisbury Steaks:

- 1 pound ground beef
- 1/4 cup bread crumbs (plain or seasoned)
- 1/4 cup onion, finely chopped
- 1/4 cup milk
- 1 egg, beaten
- 1 tablespoon Worcestershire sauce
- 1 teaspoon garlic powder
- 1/2 teaspoon salt
- 1/2 teaspoon black pepper
- 2 tablespoons vegetable oil (for frying)

For the Gravy:

- 1/2 cup onion, finely chopped
- 2 cloves garlic, minced
- 1 cup beef broth
- 1 cup water
- 2 tablespoons flour (for thickening)
- 2 tablespoons soy sauce
- 1 tablespoon Worcestershire sauce
- 1 teaspoon dried thyme
- Salt and black pepper to taste

Instructions:

1. Prepare the Salisbury Steaks:

1. **Combine Ingredients:** In a large bowl, mix together the ground beef, bread crumbs, chopped onion, milk, beaten egg, Worcestershire sauce, garlic powder, salt, and pepper. Mix until just combined; do not overmix.
2. **Form Patties:** Divide the mixture into 4-6 portions and shape each portion into oval or round patties.

2. Cook the Salisbury Steaks:

1. **Heat Oil:** In a large skillet, heat the vegetable oil over medium-high heat.
2. **Cook Patties:** Add the patties to the skillet and cook for 4-5 minutes on each side, or until they are browned and cooked through (internal temperature should reach 160°F or 71°C). Remove the patties from the skillet and set aside.

3. Prepare the Gravy:

1. **Sauté Onions and Garlic:** In the same skillet, add a little more oil if needed. Sauté the chopped onion until softened, about 3 minutes. Add the minced garlic and cook for an additional 1 minute.
2. **Make Gravy:** Stir in the flour and cook for 1-2 minutes to make a roux. Slowly whisk in the beef broth and water, and bring to a simmer. Stir in the soy sauce, Worcestershire sauce, dried thyme, salt, and black pepper.
3. **Thicken Gravy:** Continue to cook the gravy, stirring occasionally, until it thickens, about 5 minutes.

4. Combine and Serve:

1. **Return Patties:** Return the cooked Salisbury steaks to the skillet with the gravy. Simmer for 5-10 minutes, or until the patties are heated through and have absorbed some of the gravy flavor.
2. **Serve:** Serve the Salisbury steaks hot, smothered with the savory gravy.

Tips:

- **Meat Mixture:** For added flavor, you can mix in a little grated Parmesan cheese or finely chopped mushrooms into the beef mixture.
- **Gravy Thickness:** Adjust the thickness of the gravy by adding more flour for a thicker consistency or more broth/water for a thinner consistency.
- **Sides:** Salisbury steak pairs well with mashed potatoes, rice, or steamed vegetables.

Enjoy your homemade Salisbury Steak—a hearty and comforting dish that's sure to be a hit at the dinner table!

Baked Ziti

Ingredients:

- 1 pound ziti pasta (or penne)
- 2 tablespoons olive oil
- 1 pound ground beef (or Italian sausage, or a mix of both)
- 1 onion, chopped
- 2 cloves garlic, minced
- 1 (28-ounce) can marinara sauce (or your favorite pasta sauce)
- 1 (15-ounce) can tomato sauce
- 1/2 cup water (or red wine, optional for depth of flavor)
- 1 teaspoon dried basil
- 1 teaspoon dried oregano
- 1/2 teaspoon red pepper flakes (optional, for heat)
- Salt and black pepper to taste
- 1 cup ricotta cheese
- 1 1/2 cups shredded mozzarella cheese
- 1/2 cup grated Parmesan cheese
- 1/4 cup chopped fresh basil or parsley (optional, for garnish)

Instructions:

1. Cook the Pasta:

1. **Preheat Oven:** Preheat your oven to 375°F (190°C).
2. **Cook Pasta:** Bring a large pot of salted water to a boil. Cook the ziti according to the package instructions until al dente. Drain and set aside.

2. Prepare the Meat Sauce:

1. **Cook Meat:** In a large skillet or saucepan, heat olive oil over medium heat. Add the ground beef (or sausage) and cook until browned, breaking it apart with a spoon. Drain any excess fat.
2. **Sauté Vegetables:** Add the chopped onion and cook until softened, about 5 minutes. Add the minced garlic and cook for an additional 1 minute.
3. **Add Sauce Ingredients:** Stir in the marinara sauce, tomato sauce, and water (or red wine). Add the dried basil, oregano, red pepper flakes (if using), salt, and black pepper. Simmer the sauce for 10-15 minutes, allowing the flavors to meld together.

3. Combine Pasta and Sauce:

1. **Mix Pasta and Sauce:** In a large bowl, combine the cooked ziti with the meat sauce. Mix well.

4. Assemble the Baked Ziti:

1. **Layer Ingredients:** In a large baking dish (about 9x13 inches), spread half of the pasta mixture. Dot with half of the ricotta cheese and sprinkle with 1/2 cup of shredded mozzarella. Repeat with the remaining pasta mixture, ricotta, and another 1/2 cup of mozzarella.
2. **Top with Cheese:** Sprinkle the remaining 1/2 cup of mozzarella cheese and the grated Parmesan cheese on top.

5. Bake:

1. **Bake Ziti:** Cover the baking dish with aluminum foil and bake in the preheated oven for 25 minutes. Remove the foil and bake for an additional 10-15 minutes, or until the cheese is bubbly and golden brown.

6. Serve:

1. **Cool Slightly:** Allow the baked ziti to cool for a few minutes before serving.
2. **Garnish and Enjoy:** Garnish with chopped fresh basil or parsley if desired. Serve warm.

Tips:

- **Cheese:** For extra flavor, you can mix some shredded mozzarella into the pasta mixture before baking.
- **Vegetables:** Feel free to add cooked vegetables like mushrooms, bell peppers, or spinach to the meat sauce for added nutrition.
- **Make Ahead:** Baked ziti can be assembled ahead of time and stored in the refrigerator for up to 24 hours before baking. Add a few extra minutes to the baking time if baking from cold.

Enjoy your homemade Baked Ziti—a comforting and hearty dish that's always a crowd-pleaser!

Chicken Pot Pie

Ingredients:

For the Filling:

- 2 tablespoons butter
- 1 medium onion, chopped
- 2 cloves garlic, minced
- 2 medium carrots, diced
- 2 celery stalks, diced
- 1 cup frozen peas
- **2 cups cooked chicken**, diced (use rotisserie chicken or cooked chicken breasts/thighs)
- 1/3 cup all-purpose flour
- 1 1/2 cups chicken broth
- 1 cup milk (whole or 2%)
- 1 teaspoon dried thyme
- 1/2 teaspoon dried rosemary
- Salt and black pepper to taste

For the Crust:

- **1 package (14.1 ounces) refrigerated pie crusts** (or homemade pie crust if preferred)
- **1 egg, beaten** (for egg wash)

Instructions:

1. Prepare the Filling:

1. **Sauté Vegetables:** In a large skillet or saucepan, melt the butter over medium heat. Add the chopped onion, garlic, carrots, and celery. Cook until the vegetables are tender, about 5-7 minutes.
2. **Add Flour:** Stir in the flour and cook for 1-2 minutes to form a roux, which will help thicken the filling.
3. **Add Liquids:** Gradually whisk in the chicken broth and milk, ensuring there are no lumps. Cook until the mixture starts to thicken, about 5 minutes.
4. **Add Chicken and Seasoning:** Stir in the cooked chicken, frozen peas, dried thyme, dried rosemary, salt, and black pepper. Cook for a few more minutes until the mixture is heated through and thickened. Remove from heat.

2. Assemble the Pie:

1. **Preheat Oven:** Preheat your oven to 425°F (220°C).
2. **Prepare Crust:** Roll out one of the pie crusts and fit it into a 9-inch pie dish. Trim the edges.
3. **Add Filling:** Pour the chicken mixture into the prepared pie crust.

4. **Top with Crust:** Roll out the second pie crust and place it over the filling. Trim and crimp the edges to seal. Cut a few slits in the top crust to allow steam to escape.
5. **Brush with Egg Wash:** Brush the top crust with the beaten egg for a golden finish.

3. Bake:

1. **Bake Pie:** Place the pie on a baking sheet to catch any drips. Bake in the preheated oven for 30-35 minutes, or until the crust is golden brown and the filling is bubbling.
2. **Cool Slightly:** Allow the pie to cool for 5-10 minutes before serving to let the filling set.

Tips:

- **Chicken:** Use leftover cooked chicken or rotisserie chicken for convenience. You can also use turkey or even a mix of different proteins.
- **Vegetables:** Feel free to add other vegetables like corn, green beans, or mushrooms to the filling.
- **Crust:** If you prefer a flaky homemade crust, use your favorite pie crust recipe or make a double batch for a top and bottom crust.

Enjoy your homemade Chicken Pot Pie—a classic comfort dish that's sure to be a family favorite!

Scalloped Potatoes

Ingredients:

For the Filling:

- 2 tablespoons butter
- 1 medium onion, chopped
- 2 cloves garlic, minced
- 2 medium carrots, diced
- 2 celery stalks, diced
- 1 cup frozen peas
- 2 cups cooked chicken, diced (use rotisserie chicken or cooked chicken breasts/thighs)
- 1/3 cup all-purpose flour
- 1 1/2 cups chicken broth
- 1 cup milk (whole or 2%)
- 1 teaspoon dried thyme
- 1/2 teaspoon dried rosemary
- Salt and black pepper to taste

For the Crust:

- 1 package (14.1 ounces) refrigerated pie crusts (or homemade pie crust if preferred)
- 1 egg, beaten (for egg wash)

Instructions:

1. Prepare the Filling:

1. **Sauté Vegetables:** In a large skillet or saucepan, melt the butter over medium heat. Add the chopped onion, garlic, carrots, and celery. Cook until the vegetables are tender, about 5-7 minutes.
2. **Add Flour:** Stir in the flour and cook for 1-2 minutes to form a roux, which will help thicken the filling.
3. **Add Liquids:** Gradually whisk in the chicken broth and milk, ensuring there are no lumps. Cook until the mixture starts to thicken, about 5 minutes.
4. **Add Chicken and Seasoning:** Stir in the cooked chicken, frozen peas, dried thyme, dried rosemary, salt, and black pepper. Cook for a few more minutes until the mixture is heated through and thickened. Remove from heat.

2. Assemble the Pie:

1. **Preheat Oven:** Preheat your oven to 425°F (220°C).
2. **Prepare Crust:** Roll out one of the pie crusts and fit it into a 9-inch pie dish. Trim the edges.
3. **Add Filling:** Pour the chicken mixture into the prepared pie crust.
4. **Top with Crust:** Roll out the second pie crust and place it over the filling. Trim and crimp the edges to seal. Cut a few slits in the top crust to allow steam to escape.

5. **Brush with Egg Wash:** Brush the top crust with the beaten egg for a golden finish.

3. Bake:

1. **Bake Pie:** Place the pie on a baking sheet to catch any drips. Bake in the preheated oven for 30-35 minutes, or until the crust is golden brown and the filling is bubbling.
2. **Cool Slightly:** Allow the pie to cool for 5-10 minutes before serving to let the filling set.

Tips:

- **Chicken:** Use leftover cooked chicken or rotisserie chicken for convenience. You can also use turkey or even a mix of different proteins.
- **Vegetables:** Feel free to add other vegetables like corn, green beans, or mushrooms to the filling.
- **Crust:** If you prefer a flaky homemade crust, use your favorite pie crust recipe or make a double batch for a top and bottom crust.

Enjoy your homemade Chicken Pot Pie—a classic comfort dish that's sure to be a family favorite!

Scalloped Potatoes

Ingredients:

- **4 large russet potatoes**, peeled and thinly sliced (about 1/8-inch thick)
- **2 tablespoons butter**
- **1 small onion**, finely chopped
- **2 cloves garlic**, minced
- **3 tablespoons all-purpose flour**
- **2 cups whole milk**
- **1 cup heavy cream**
- **1 1/2 cups shredded cheddar cheese** (sharp or mild, depending on preference)
- **1/2 teaspoon dried thyme** (or 1 teaspoon fresh thyme, chopped)
- **1/4 teaspoon paprika**
- **Salt and black pepper to taste**
- **1/4 cup grated Parmesan cheese** (optional, for extra flavor)

Instructions:

1. Preheat Oven:

1. **Preheat Oven:** Preheat your oven to 375°F (190°C).

2. Prepare the Sauce:

1. **Sauté Onions and Garlic:** In a medium saucepan, melt the butter over medium heat. Add the finely chopped onion and cook until softened, about 5 minutes. Add the minced garlic and cook for an additional 1 minute.
2. **Make Roux:** Stir in the flour and cook for 1-2 minutes to form a roux, which will help thicken the sauce.
3. **Add Liquids:** Gradually whisk in the milk and heavy cream, making sure to smooth out any lumps. Continue to cook and stir until the mixture starts to thicken, about 5-7 minutes.
4. **Add Cheese and Seasoning:** Stir in the shredded cheddar cheese, dried thyme, paprika, salt, and black pepper. Cook until the cheese is melted and the sauce is smooth.

3. Assemble the Dish:

1. **Layer Potatoes:** Arrange a layer of thinly sliced potatoes in the bottom of a greased 9x13-inch baking dish. Season with a bit of salt and pepper.
2. **Add Sauce:** Pour a portion of the cheese sauce over the potatoes. Repeat the layering process until all potatoes and sauce are used, finishing with a layer of cheese sauce on top.
3. **Top with Parmesan:** If using, sprinkle the grated Parmesan cheese on top.

4. Bake:

1. **Cover and Bake:** Cover the baking dish with aluminum foil and bake in the preheated oven for 45 minutes.

2. **Uncover and Continue Baking:** Remove the foil and bake for an additional 15-20 minutes, or until the potatoes are tender and the top is golden brown and bubbly.
3. **Cool Slightly:** Let the scalloped potatoes cool for 5-10 minutes before serving to allow the sauce to set.

Tips:

- **Potatoes:** Russet potatoes work best for this dish because they become tender and creamy when baked. Make sure the slices are evenly cut for even cooking.
- **Creaminess:** For a richer dish, use all heavy cream instead of a mix of milk and cream.
- **Variation:** Add other ingredients like cooked bacon bits, caramelized onions, or additional herbs for extra flavor.

Enjoy your creamy and cheesy Scalloped Potatoes—a perfect side dish that's sure to be a hit at your table!

Chicken Casserole

Ingredients:

- **2 cups cooked chicken**, shredded or diced (rotisserie chicken works great)
- **1 cup cooked rice** (white or brown)
- **1 can (10.5 ounces) cream of chicken soup** (or homemade)
- **1/2 cup sour cream**
- **1 cup frozen peas and carrots** (or mixed vegetables of your choice)
- **1/2 cup milk**
- **1 cup shredded cheddar cheese** (or your preferred cheese)
- **1/4 cup finely chopped onion** (optional)
- **1/4 teaspoon garlic powder**
- **1/4 teaspoon paprika**
- **Salt and black pepper to taste**
- **1/2 cup crushed butter crackers** (such as Ritz) or breadcrumbs
- **2 tablespoons melted butter** (for topping)

Instructions:

1. Preheat Oven:

1. **Preheat Oven:** Preheat your oven to 375°F (190°C).

2. Prepare the Casserole Mixture:

1. **Mix Ingredients:** In a large bowl, combine the cooked chicken, cooked rice, cream of chicken soup, sour cream, frozen peas and carrots, milk, shredded cheddar cheese, chopped onion (if using), garlic powder, paprika, salt, and black pepper. Mix well until all ingredients are evenly combined.

3. Assemble the Casserole:

1. **Transfer to Baking Dish:** Pour the mixture into a greased 9x13-inch baking dish, spreading it out evenly.
2. **Prepare Topping:** In a small bowl, mix the crushed butter crackers or breadcrumbs with melted butter. Sprinkle this mixture evenly over the top of the casserole.

4. Bake:

1. **Bake Casserole:** Bake in the preheated oven for 30-35 minutes, or until the casserole is bubbly and the topping is golden brown.
2. **Cool Slightly:** Allow the casserole to cool for a few minutes before serving.

Tips:

- **Vegetables:** Feel free to use your favorite vegetables or add extras like mushrooms, bell peppers, or corn.
- **Cheese:** Experiment with different cheeses like mozzarella, Monterey Jack, or a blend for varied flavors.

- **Make Ahead:** This casserole can be assembled ahead of time and refrigerated for up to 24 hours before baking. Add a few extra minutes to the baking time if baking from cold.
- **Freezing:** You can also freeze the unbaked casserole for up to 3 months. Thaw in the refrigerator overnight before baking.

Enjoy your hearty and comforting Chicken Casserole—a perfect meal for any occasion!

Cowboy Beans

Ingredients:

- **1 pound dried pinto beans** (or 4 cups canned pinto beans, drained and rinsed)
- **1/2 pound bacon**, chopped
- **1/2 pound ground beef** (optional, for extra richness)
- **1 large onion**, chopped
- **2 cloves garlic**, minced
- **1 bell pepper**, chopped (any color)
- **1 (15-ounce) can tomato sauce**
- **1/2 cup barbecue sauce**
- **1/4 cup brown sugar**
- **2 tablespoons molasses**
- **1 tablespoon Worcestershire sauce**
- **1 teaspoon smoked paprika**
- **1/2 teaspoon chili powder**
- **1/2 teaspoon ground cumin**
- **Salt and black pepper to taste**
- **1 cup water** (or more as needed)

Instructions:

1. Prepare the Beans:

1. **Soak Beans:** If using dried beans, rinse them under cold water. Place the beans in a large bowl and cover with water. Soak overnight or use the quick soak method: bring the beans and water to a boil, then remove from heat and let them sit for 1 hour. Drain and rinse.
2. **Cook Beans:** In a large pot, cover the soaked beans with fresh water. Bring to a boil, then reduce the heat and simmer for 1-1.5 hours, or until the beans are tender. Drain and set aside.

2. Prepare the Meat and Vegetables:

1. **Cook Bacon:** In a large skillet or pot, cook the chopped bacon over medium heat until crispy. Remove the bacon with a slotted spoon and set aside, leaving the bacon fat in the skillet.
2. **Cook Beef:** If using ground beef, add it to the skillet with the bacon fat. Cook until browned, breaking it up with a spoon. Drain excess fat if necessary.
3. **Sauté Vegetables:** Add the chopped onion, garlic, and bell pepper to the skillet. Cook until the vegetables are softened, about 5 minutes.

3. Combine Ingredients:

1. **Mix Ingredients:** In a large pot or Dutch oven, combine the cooked beans, bacon, ground beef (if using), sautéed vegetables, tomato sauce, barbecue sauce, brown sugar, molasses, Worcestershire sauce, smoked paprika, chili powder, ground cumin, salt, and black pepper. Stir well.

2. **Add Water:** Add 1 cup of water to the mixture. Stir to combine. Add more water if needed to reach your desired consistency.

4. Simmer:

1. **Simmer Beans:** Bring the mixture to a boil, then reduce the heat to low. Cover and simmer for 30-45 minutes, stirring occasionally. The beans should be thick and flavorful. Adjust seasoning as needed.

5. Serve:

1. **Serve Hot:** Serve the Cowboy Beans hot as a hearty side dish or main course.

Tips:

- **Beans:** If using canned beans, reduce the cooking time and skip the soaking step. Simply combine all ingredients and simmer until flavors meld.
- **Meat:** You can also add other meats like diced ham or sausage for added flavor.
- **Sweetness and Smokiness:** Adjust the amount of brown sugar, molasses, and smoked paprika to suit your taste preference.

Enjoy your Cowboy Beans—a delicious and satisfying dish that's perfect for a crowd or a cozy family dinner!

Garlic Mashed Potatoes

Ingredients:

- **2 pounds russet potatoes**, peeled and cut into chunks
- **4 cloves garlic**, peeled (or more if you like a stronger garlic flavor)
- **1/2 cup milk** (whole or 2%)
- **1/4 cup heavy cream**
- **1/4 cup unsalted butter**, cut into pieces
- **Salt and black pepper to taste**
- **Chopped fresh parsley** (optional, for garnish)

Instructions:

1. Cook the Potatoes and Garlic:

1. **Boil Potatoes and Garlic:** Place the peeled and cut potatoes, along with the garlic cloves, in a large pot. Cover with cold water and add a pinch of salt. Bring to a boil over high heat. Reduce the heat to medium and simmer until the potatoes are tender and easily pierced with a fork, about 15-20 minutes.
2. **Drain:** Drain the potatoes and garlic well in a colander.

2. Mash the Potatoes and Garlic:

1. **Mash Potatoes and Garlic:** Return the drained potatoes and garlic to the pot or a large bowl. Use a potato masher to mash them until smooth. For an extra creamy texture, you can use a potato ricer or food mill.

3. Add Cream and Butter:

1. **Heat Cream and Butter:** In a small saucepan, combine the milk, heavy cream, and butter. Heat over medium heat until the butter is melted and the mixture is warm (do not boil).
2. **Combine:** Gradually add the warm cream and butter mixture to the mashed potatoes, stirring until smooth and creamy. Adjust the amount of liquid to reach your desired consistency.

4. Season and Serve:

1. **Season:** Season with salt and black pepper to taste. Stir well to combine.
2. **Garnish:** Transfer the mashed potatoes to a serving dish. Garnish with chopped fresh parsley if desired.

Tips:

- **Garlic:** For a milder garlic flavor, you can roast the garlic before adding it to the potatoes. To do this, cut the top off a garlic bulb, drizzle with olive oil, wrap in foil, and roast at 400°F (200°C) for 30-35 minutes until soft. Squeeze the roasted garlic cloves out of their skins and mash them into the potatoes.

- **Consistency:** Adjust the amount of milk and cream to make the mashed potatoes as creamy or chunky as you prefer.
- **Butter:** For extra richness, you can increase the amount of butter or use half-and-half instead of milk and cream.

Enjoy your Garlic Mashed Potatoes—a delicious, comforting side dish that pairs well with a variety of main courses!

Southern Cornbread Dressing

Ingredients:

For the Cornbread:

- 1 cup cornmeal
- 1 cup all-purpose flour
- 1 tablespoon baking powder
- 1/2 teaspoon salt
- 1 cup buttermilk
- 2 large eggs
- 1/4 cup vegetable oil (or melted butter)
- 1 cup cooked and crumbled bacon (optional, for added flavor)

For the Dressing:

- 1 tablespoon butter
- 1 large onion, chopped
- 2 celery stalks, chopped
- 2 cloves garlic, minced
- 1/4 cup fresh parsley, chopped (or 2 tablespoons dried parsley)
- 1 teaspoon dried sage
- 1 teaspoon dried thyme
- 1/2 teaspoon dried rosemary (optional)
- 2 cups chicken or vegetable broth
- 1 large egg, beaten
- **Salt and black pepper to taste

Instructions:

1. Prepare the Cornbread:

1. **Preheat Oven:** Preheat your oven to 425°F (220°C).
2. **Mix Dry Ingredients:** In a large bowl, whisk together the cornmeal, flour, baking powder, and salt.
3. **Mix Wet Ingredients:** In another bowl, combine the buttermilk, eggs, and vegetable oil (or melted butter).
4. **Combine:** Pour the wet ingredients into the dry ingredients and stir until just combined. Fold in the crumbled bacon if using.
5. **Bake:** Pour the batter into a greased 8x8-inch baking dish or cast-iron skillet. Bake for 20-25 minutes, or until the cornbread is golden brown and a toothpick inserted into the center comes out clean. Let it cool, then crumble into pieces for the dressing.

2. Prepare the Dressing:

1. **Sauté Vegetables:** In a large skillet, melt the butter over medium heat. Add the chopped onion and celery, and cook until softened, about 5-7 minutes. Add the minced garlic and cook for an additional 1 minute. Remove from heat.

2. **Combine Ingredients:** In a large bowl, combine the crumbled cornbread, sautéed vegetables, parsley, sage, thyme, rosemary (if using), and salt and black pepper.
3. **Add Broth and Egg:** Gradually add the chicken or vegetable broth, mixing until the dressing is moist but not soggy. Stir in the beaten egg.
4. **Adjust Seasoning:** Taste and adjust seasoning as needed. If the mixture seems dry, add a bit more broth.

3. Bake the Dressing:

1. **Prepare Baking Dish:** Transfer the dressing mixture to a greased 9x13-inch baking dish or a similarly sized dish.
2. **Bake:** Bake in the preheated oven at 375°F (190°C) for 30-35 minutes, or until the top is golden brown and the dressing is heated through.

Tips:

- **Make Ahead:** The cornbread and dressing mixture can be prepared a day in advance. Store the cornbread in an airtight container and the dressing mixture in the refrigerator until ready to bake.
- **Additions:** Feel free to add other ingredients such as cooked sausage, mushrooms, or nuts for added texture and flavor.
- **Moisture:** If the dressing seems too dry before baking, add a little extra broth to achieve the desired consistency.

Enjoy your Southern Cornbread Dressing—a delicious and traditional side dish that complements any hearty meal!

Green Bean Casserole

Ingredients:

- **2 cans (14.5 ounces each) green beans**, drained (or about 4 cups fresh green beans, trimmed and cut into bite-sized pieces)
- **1 can (10.5 ounces) cream of mushroom soup** (or homemade)
- **1/2 cup milk**
- **1 cup shredded cheddar cheese** (optional, for extra creaminess)
- **1/2 teaspoon soy sauce**
- **1/4 teaspoon black pepper**
- **1/4 teaspoon garlic powder**
- **1/4 teaspoon onion powder**
- **1 cup French fried onions** (store-bought or homemade)
- **1/2 cup sliced almonds** (optional, for added crunch)

Instructions:

1. Preheat Oven:

1. **Preheat Oven:** Preheat your oven to 350°F (175°C).

2. Prepare the Casserole Mixture:

1. **Mix Ingredients:** In a large bowl, combine the cream of mushroom soup, milk, shredded cheddar cheese (if using), soy sauce, black pepper, garlic powder, and onion powder. Stir until well combined.
2. **Add Green Beans:** Add the green beans to the mixture and stir to coat the beans evenly.

3. Assemble the Casserole:

1. **Transfer to Baking Dish:** Pour the green bean mixture into a greased 9x13-inch baking dish or a similarly sized casserole dish.
2. **Top with Fried Onions:** Sprinkle the French fried onions evenly over the top of the casserole. If using sliced almonds, sprinkle them on top as well.

4. Bake:

1. **Bake Casserole:** Bake in the preheated oven for 30-35 minutes, or until the casserole is hot and bubbly, and the fried onions are golden brown and crispy.
2. **Cool Slightly:** Allow the casserole to cool for a few minutes before serving.

Tips:

- **Fresh Green Beans:** If using fresh green beans, blanch them in boiling water for 3-4 minutes until tender-crisp before mixing with the sauce.
- **Homemade Soup:** For a homemade version, use a recipe for cream of mushroom soup or substitute with other creamy soups like cream of celery.

- **Crispy Topping:** To keep the fried onions crispy, you can add them during the last 10 minutes of baking if they start to brown too quickly.

Enjoy your Green Bean Casserole—a classic side dish that's creamy, flavorful, and perfect for any occasion!

Chicken Parmesan

Ingredients:

For the Chicken:

- 4 boneless, skinless chicken breasts
- Salt and black pepper to taste
- 1 cup all-purpose flour
- 2 large eggs
- 1 cup breadcrumbs (Italian or plain)
- 1 cup grated Parmesan cheese
- 1 cup marinara sauce (store-bought or homemade)
- 1 1/2 cups shredded mozzarella cheese
- 1/4 cup chopped fresh basil (optional, for garnish)
- 2 tablespoons olive oil (or vegetable oil)

For the Marinara Sauce (if homemade):

- 1 tablespoon olive oil
- 1 small onion, chopped
- 2 cloves garlic, minced
- 1 can (15 ounces) crushed tomatoes
- 1 teaspoon dried basil
- 1/2 teaspoon dried oregano
- 1/2 teaspoon sugar (optional, to balance acidity)
- Salt and black pepper to taste

Instructions:

1. Prepare the Marinara Sauce (if making homemade):

1. **Sauté Onions and Garlic:** In a medium saucepan, heat the olive oil over medium heat. Add the chopped onion and cook until softened, about 5 minutes. Add the minced garlic and cook for another minute.
2. **Add Tomatoes and Seasoning:** Stir in the crushed tomatoes, dried basil, dried oregano, sugar (if using), salt, and black pepper. Bring to a simmer and cook for 15-20 minutes, stirring occasionally. Adjust seasoning as needed.

2. Prepare the Chicken:

1. **Pound Chicken:** Place the chicken breasts between two sheets of plastic wrap or parchment paper. Use a meat mallet or rolling pin to gently pound them to an even thickness (about 1/2-inch thick). This ensures even cooking.
2. **Season:** Season the chicken breasts with salt and black pepper on both sides.

3. Bread the Chicken:

1. **Set Up Dredging Station:** Place the flour in a shallow dish. In another shallow dish, beat the eggs. In a third shallow dish, combine the breadcrumbs and grated Parmesan cheese.
2. **Dredge Chicken:** Dredge each chicken breast in the flour, shaking off excess. Dip in the beaten eggs, then coat with the breadcrumb mixture, pressing gently to adhere.

4. Cook the Chicken:

1. **Heat Oil:** In a large skillet, heat the olive oil over medium heat.
2. **Cook Chicken:** Add the breaded chicken breasts to the skillet and cook until golden brown and cooked through, about 4-5 minutes per side. Transfer the chicken to a paper towel-lined plate to drain.

5. Assemble and Bake:

1. **Preheat Oven:** Preheat your oven to 375°F (190°C).
2. **Add Sauce and Cheese:** Spread a thin layer of marinara sauce on the bottom of a baking dish. Place the cooked chicken breasts in the dish. Spoon additional marinara sauce over each piece of chicken. Sprinkle shredded mozzarella cheese on top.
3. **Bake:** Bake in the preheated oven for 20-25 minutes, or until the cheese is melted and bubbly and the chicken is heated through.

6. Garnish and Serve:

1. **Garnish:** Sprinkle with chopped fresh basil, if desired.
2. **Serve:** Serve the Chicken Parmesan with your choice of pasta, garlic bread, or a fresh green salad.

Tips:

- **Chicken Tenderness:** For extra tender chicken, consider marinating it in buttermilk for a few hours before breading.
- **Cheese:** You can use other cheeses like provolone or a blend for different flavors.
- **Make Ahead:** The chicken can be breaded and cooked in advance, then assembled with sauce and cheese before baking.

Enjoy your Chicken Parmesan—a delicious, satisfying dish that's sure to please everyone at the table!

Pork Tenderloin

Ingredients:

- **2 pork tenderloins** (about 1 pound each)
- **2 tablespoons olive oil**
- **2 cloves garlic**, minced
- **1 tablespoon fresh rosemary**, chopped (or 1 teaspoon dried rosemary)
- **1 tablespoon fresh thyme**, chopped (or 1 teaspoon dried thyme)
- **1 tablespoon Dijon mustard**
- **1 tablespoon soy sauce**
- **1 tablespoon brown sugar**
- ****Salt and black pepper to taste**

Instructions:

1. Preheat Oven:

1. **Preheat Oven:** Preheat your oven to 400°F (200°C).

2. Prepare the Marinade:

1. **Mix Marinade:** In a small bowl, combine the olive oil, minced garlic, chopped rosemary, chopped thyme, Dijon mustard, soy sauce, brown sugar, salt, and black pepper. Mix well.

3. Prepare the Pork Tenderloin:

1. **Trim Tenderloin:** If needed, trim any excess fat or silver skin from the pork tenderloins.
2. **Apply Marinade:** Rub the marinade all over the pork tenderloins, making sure to coat them evenly. You can let them marinate for 30 minutes to 2 hours in the refrigerator if you have time, but this step is optional.

4. Roast the Pork:

1. **Sear Tenderloin:** Heat a large oven-safe skillet over medium-high heat. Add a little olive oil if needed. Sear the pork tenderloins on all sides until browned, about 2-3 minutes per side.
2. **Transfer to Oven:** Transfer the skillet to the preheated oven.
3. **Roast:** Roast the pork tenderloins for 15-20 minutes, or until an internal thermometer inserted into the thickest part of the meat reads 145°F (63°C). The exact cooking time may vary depending on the size and thickness of the tenderloins.

5. Rest and Serve:

1. **Rest Meat:** Remove the skillet from the oven and transfer the pork tenderloins to a cutting board. Let them rest for 5-10 minutes before slicing. This helps the juices redistribute and keeps the meat moist.
2. **Slice:** Slice the pork tenderloins into medallions and serve.

Tips:

- **Marinating:** If you have time, marinating the pork tenderloin in the refrigerator for a few hours or overnight will enhance the flavor.
- **Searing:** Searing the pork tenderloin before roasting adds a nice caramelization and depth of flavor.
- **Sauce:** Consider deglazing the skillet with a splash of white wine or chicken broth after removing the pork to create a quick sauce. Scrape up any browned bits and simmer until slightly reduced.

Enjoy your Roasted Pork Tenderloin—a tender, flavorful dish that pairs well with a variety of sides like roasted vegetables, mashed potatoes, or a fresh salad!

Cheesy Grits

Ingredients:

- **1 cup grits** (stone-ground or quick grits)
- **4 cups water** (or a mix of water and milk for creamier grits)
- **1 teaspoon salt**
- **1/2 cup milk** (optional, for creamier grits)
- **2 tablespoons butter**
- **1 cup shredded sharp cheddar cheese** (or your favorite cheese)
- **1/4 cup grated Parmesan cheese** (optional, for extra flavor)
- **Black pepper to taste**
- **Chopped fresh parsley** (optional, for garnish)

Instructions:

1. Cook the Grits:

1. **Boil Water:** In a large pot, bring 4 cups of water to a boil. Add the salt.
2. **Add Grits:** Gradually whisk in the grits, reducing the heat to low.
3. **Simmer:** Cover and cook the grits, stirring occasionally, according to the package instructions (usually about 20-25 minutes for stone-ground grits or 5-10 minutes for quick grits). Stir frequently to prevent lumps and sticking.

2. Add Creaminess and Cheese:

1. **Stir in Milk (Optional):** If using, stir in the milk during the last 5 minutes of cooking for creamier grits.
2. **Add Butter:** Once the grits are cooked and creamy, stir in the butter until melted and well combined.
3. **Add Cheese:** Gradually mix in the shredded cheddar cheese and Parmesan cheese (if using), stirring until the cheese is fully melted and the grits are smooth.
4. **Season:** Taste and adjust seasoning with black pepper as needed.

3. Serve:

1. **Garnish:** Garnish with chopped fresh parsley if desired.
2. **Serve Hot:** Serve the cheesy grits hot as a side dish or a standalone breakfast.

Tips:

- **Consistency:** Adjust the consistency of the grits by adding more milk or water if they become too thick. They should be creamy and smooth.
- **Cheese Variety:** Feel free to experiment with different cheeses such as Gouda, Monterey Jack, or a blend of cheeses for varied flavors.
- **Add-Ins:** You can enhance the grits with additional ingredients like cooked bacon, sautéed mushrooms, or a sprinkle of hot sauce for extra flavor.

Enjoy your Cheesy Grits—a comforting and indulgent dish that's sure to be a hit at your table!

Bacon-Wrapped Meatloaf

Ingredients:

For the Meatloaf:

- 1 pound ground beef
- 1/2 pound ground pork
- 1/2 cup breadcrumbs (or crushed crackers)
- 1/2 cup milk
- 1/4 cup ketchup
- 1/4 cup finely chopped onion
- 1 clove garlic, minced
- 1 large egg
- 1 tablespoon Worcestershire sauce
- 1 teaspoon dried thyme
- 1 teaspoon dried oregano
- 1/2 teaspoon salt
- 1/2 teaspoon black pepper

For the Bacon Wrap:

- 8-10 slices bacon (enough to cover the meatloaf)

For the Glaze (optional):

- 1/4 cup ketchup
- 2 tablespoons brown sugar
- 1 tablespoon Worcestershire sauce

Instructions:

1. Preheat Oven:

1. **Preheat Oven:** Preheat your oven to 375°F (190°C).

2. Prepare the Meatloaf Mixture:

1. **Mix Ingredients:** In a large bowl, combine the ground beef, ground pork, breadcrumbs, milk, ketchup, chopped onion, minced garlic, egg, Worcestershire sauce, dried thyme, dried oregano, salt, and black pepper. Mix until just combined, being careful not to overmix.

3. Shape the Meatloaf:

1. **Form Meatloaf:** Transfer the meat mixture to a baking sheet or a loaf pan. Shape into a loaf, about 6 inches wide and 8 inches long.

4. Wrap with Bacon:

1. **Wrap with Bacon:** Lay the bacon slices over the meatloaf, slightly overlapping each slice and tucking the ends underneath the meatloaf. You may need to adjust the number of bacon slices based on the size of your meatloaf.

5. Bake the Meatloaf:

1. **Bake:** Place the meatloaf in the preheated oven and bake for 45-55 minutes, or until the internal temperature reaches 160°F (71°C). The bacon should be crispy and the meatloaf should be cooked through.

6. Add Glaze (Optional):

1. **Prepare Glaze:** While the meatloaf is baking, mix together the ketchup, brown sugar, and Worcestershire sauce in a small bowl.
2. **Glaze Meatloaf:** In the last 10 minutes of baking, brush the glaze over the meatloaf. Return to the oven and bake until the glaze is bubbly and slightly caramelized.

7. Rest and Serve:

1. **Rest Meatloaf:** Remove the meatloaf from the oven and let it rest for 10 minutes before slicing. This helps the juices redistribute and makes for easier slicing.
2. **Slice and Serve:** Slice the meatloaf and serve with your favorite sides.

Tips:

- **Bacon Crispiness:** If the bacon isn't as crispy as you'd like, you can put the meatloaf under the broiler for a few minutes, keeping a close eye on it to prevent burning.
- **Lean Meat:** Use a mix of lean and slightly fatty meat to keep the meatloaf moist and flavorful.
- **Variations:** Add other ingredients like chopped bell peppers, mushrooms, or shredded cheese to the meat mixture for extra flavor.

Enjoy your Bacon-Wrapped Meatloaf—a hearty, flavorful dish with a savory bacon twist!

Country Ham

Ingredients:

- **1 whole country ham** (about 8-10 pounds, bone-in or boneless)
- **Water** (enough to cover the ham)
- **1 cup brown sugar**
- **1/2 cup honey**
- **1/2 cup Dijon mustard**
- **1/4 cup apple cider vinegar**
- **Whole cloves** (optional, for studding)

Instructions:

1. Prepare the Ham:

1. **Soak the Ham:** If your ham is very salty, soak it in water for 12-24 hours, changing the water every 4-6 hours to help reduce the saltiness. This step is optional but recommended for very salty hams.
2. **Preheat Oven:** Preheat your oven to 325°F (163°C).

2. Bake the Ham:

1. **Prepare Ham:** If the ham is not pre-sliced, score the surface in a diamond pattern with a sharp knife. This helps the glaze penetrate the meat. Optionally, you can stud the ham with whole cloves by inserting them into the intersections of the diamond pattern.
2. **Place in Roasting Pan:** Place the ham in a large roasting pan. Add enough water to cover the bottom of the pan to keep the ham moist during cooking.
3. **Cover:** Cover the ham with aluminum foil or a lid to retain moisture.

3. Bake:

1. **Bake:** Bake the ham in the preheated oven for about 15-18 minutes per pound. For an 8-10 pound ham, this will be approximately 2-2.5 hours. The internal temperature should reach 140°F (60°C).

4. Glaze the Ham:

1. **Prepare Glaze:** While the ham is baking, prepare the glaze by combining brown sugar, honey, Dijon mustard, and apple cider vinegar in a bowl. Mix until smooth.
2. **Apply Glaze:** About 30 minutes before the ham is done, remove it from the oven and brush a generous amount of glaze over the surface of the ham.
3. **Continue Baking:** Return the ham to the oven, uncovered, and bake for the remaining time, basting with the glaze every 10-15 minutes until the glaze is caramelized and the ham reaches an internal temperature of 140°F (60°C).

5. Rest and Serve:

1. **Rest Ham:** Remove the ham from the oven and let it rest for 15-20 minutes before slicing. This helps the juices redistribute and makes for easier slicing.
2. **Slice and Serve:** Slice the ham thinly and serve.

Tips:

- **Basting:** Basting the ham with the glaze several times during the last 30 minutes of baking helps develop a delicious, sticky coating.
- **Flavor Variations:** You can add spices or fruit juices to the glaze for different flavors, such as adding a pinch of ground cloves or a splash of orange juice.
- **Leftovers:** Country ham can be used in a variety of dishes, from sandwiches to soups, and makes excellent leftovers.

Enjoy your Baked Country Ham—a classic and flavorful dish that's perfect for special occasions or holiday meals!

Fried Catfish

Ingredients:

- **4 catfish fillets** (about 1 pound, thawed if frozen)
- **1 cup buttermilk** (or milk with a tablespoon of vinegar as a substitute)
- **1 cup cornmeal**
- **1/2 cup all-purpose flour**
- **1 tablespoon paprika**
- **1 teaspoon garlic powder**
- **1 teaspoon onion powder**
- **1/2 teaspoon cayenne pepper** (optional, for a bit of heat)
- **1 teaspoon salt**
- **1/2 teaspoon black pepper**
- **Vegetable oil** (for frying)

Instructions:

1. Prepare the Catfish:

1. **Marinate:** Place the catfish fillets in a shallow dish and pour the buttermilk over them. Allow the fillets to marinate for at least 30 minutes in the refrigerator. This helps tenderize the fish and adds flavor.

2. Prepare the Coating:

1. **Mix Dry Ingredients:** In a large bowl, combine the cornmeal, flour, paprika, garlic powder, onion powder, cayenne pepper (if using), salt, and black pepper. Mix well to combine.

3. Coat the Catfish:

1. **Dredge Fillets:** Remove the catfish fillets from the buttermilk, allowing excess to drip off. Dredge each fillet in the cornmeal mixture, pressing lightly to ensure the coating sticks. For extra crispy fish, double coat by dipping the fillets back into the buttermilk and then dredging in the cornmeal mixture again.

4. Fry the Catfish:

1. **Heat Oil:** In a large skillet or deep fryer, heat about 1/2 inch of vegetable oil over medium-high heat until hot (around 350°F or 175°C). To test if the oil is ready, drop a small pinch of the coating into the oil; it should sizzle and float.
2. **Fry Fillets:** Carefully add the coated catfish fillets to the hot oil, cooking in batches if necessary to avoid overcrowding. Fry for 4-6 minutes per side, or until the coating is golden brown and the fish is cooked through (the internal temperature should reach 145°F or 63°C). Use a slotted spoon or tongs to turn the fillets and remove them from the oil.
3. **Drain:** Transfer the fried catfish to a plate lined with paper towels to drain excess oil.

5. Serve:

1. **Serve Hot:** Serve the fried catfish hot with your favorite sides. Common accompaniments include coleslaw, cornbread, hushpuppies, or fries.

Tips:

- **Oil Temperature:** Maintaining the right oil temperature is key for crispy catfish. Too hot and the coating will burn; too cool and it will become soggy. Use a thermometer for accuracy.
- **Seasoning:** Adjust the seasoning in the coating to your taste, or add extra spices like Old Bay or seasoned salt for more flavor.
- **Fish Freshness:** Fresh catfish will yield the best results, but frozen fillets are a good option too. Just be sure to thaw them completely and pat them dry before coating.

Enjoy your Fried Catfish—a crispy, flavorful dish that's perfect for a comforting meal or a special occasion!

Sweet Potato Casserole

Ingredients:

For the Sweet Potato Mixture:

- **4 cups cooked sweet potatoes** (about 4 medium sweet potatoes, peeled and cubed)
- **1/2 cup granulated sugar**
- **1/2 cup packed brown sugar**
- **1/2 cup butter** (1 stick, melted)
- **2 large eggs**
- **1/4 cup milk**
- **1 teaspoon vanilla extract**
- **1/2 teaspoon ground cinnamon**
- **1/4 teaspoon ground nutmeg**
- **Pinch of salt**

For the Topping:

- **1 cup chopped pecans**
- **1/2 cup packed brown sugar**
- **1/4 cup all-purpose flour**
- **1/4 cup butter** (1/2 stick, melted)

Instructions:

1. Prepare the Sweet Potatoes:

1. **Cook Sweet Potatoes:** Peel and cube the sweet potatoes. Boil in a large pot of water until tender, about 15-20 minutes. Drain well and let cool slightly.
2. **Mash:** Mash the sweet potatoes with a potato masher or use a food processor until smooth.

2. Make the Sweet Potato Mixture:

1. **Preheat Oven:** Preheat your oven to 350°F (175°C).
2. **Mix Ingredients:** In a large bowl, combine the mashed sweet potatoes, granulated sugar, brown sugar, melted butter, eggs, milk, vanilla extract, ground cinnamon, ground nutmeg, and a pinch of salt. Mix well until smooth.
3. **Transfer to Baking Dish:** Pour the sweet potato mixture into a greased 9x13-inch baking dish or similar-sized casserole dish.

3. Prepare the Topping:

1. **Combine Topping Ingredients:** In a medium bowl, combine the chopped pecans, brown sugar, flour, and melted butter. Mix until the ingredients are well combined and form a crumbly mixture.
2. **Spread Topping:** Sprinkle the pecan topping evenly over the sweet potato mixture in the baking dish.

4. Bake:

1. **Bake Casserole:** Bake in the preheated oven for 30-35 minutes, or until the topping is golden brown and the casserole is hot and bubbly.

5. Serve:

1. **Cool Slightly:** Allow the casserole to cool for a few minutes before serving. This helps the flavors meld and makes it easier to scoop.

Tips:

- **Sweet Potatoes:** You can also use canned sweet potatoes for convenience. Just be sure to drain them well and mash before mixing with the other ingredients.
- **Topping Variations:** You can substitute pecans with walnuts or add a pinch of sea salt to the topping for a bit of contrast.
- **Make Ahead:** Prepare the sweet potato mixture and topping in advance, then refrigerate. Assemble and bake on the day you plan to serve.

Enjoy your Sweet Potato Casserole—a rich, flavorful dish that's sure to be a hit at any meal!

Potato Salad

Ingredients:

- **2 pounds potatoes** (such as Russet or Yukon Gold)
- **1 cup mayonnaise**

- **2 tablespoons Dijon mustard**
- **1 tablespoon apple cider vinegar** (or white vinegar)
- **1 tablespoon sugar** (optional, for a touch of sweetness)
- **1/2 cup finely chopped celery**
- **1/4 cup finely chopped onion** (white or red)
- **1/4 cup chopped pickles** (dill or sweet, based on preference)
- **2 large eggs**, hard-boiled and chopped
- **Salt and black pepper** to taste
- **2 tablespoons chopped fresh parsley** (optional, for garnish)
- **Paprika** (optional, for garnish)

Instructions:

1. Prepare the Potatoes:

1. **Cook Potatoes:** Peel the potatoes if desired (leaving the skin on is optional). Cut them into bite-sized cubes. Place the potatoes in a large pot and cover with cold water. Add a pinch of salt.
2. **Boil:** Bring the water to a boil over high heat, then reduce the heat to medium and cook until the potatoes are tender but not falling apart, about 10-15 minutes.
3. **Drain and Cool:** Drain the potatoes in a colander and let them cool slightly. You can also rinse them under cold water to speed up the cooling process.

2. Make the Dressing:

1. **Combine Ingredients:** In a large bowl, mix together the mayonnaise, Dijon mustard, apple cider vinegar, and sugar (if using). Stir until well combined.

3. Assemble the Salad:

1. **Mix Ingredients:** Add the slightly cooled potatoes to the bowl with the dressing. Gently fold the potatoes into the dressing to coat them evenly.
2. **Add Veggies and Eggs:** Fold in the chopped celery, onion, pickles, and hard-boiled eggs. Mix gently to combine without breaking up the potatoes.

4. Season and Garnish:

1. **Season:** Taste and adjust the seasoning with salt and black pepper as needed.
2. **Garnish:** If desired, garnish with chopped fresh parsley and a sprinkle of paprika.

5. Chill and Serve:

1. **Refrigerate:** Cover the potato salad with plastic wrap and refrigerate for at least 1-2 hours before serving. This allows the flavors to meld together.
2. **Serve:** Serve chilled and enjoy!

Tips:

- **Potato Type:** Yukon Gold potatoes are creamy and have a rich flavor, while Russet potatoes are more starchy and can become mealy if overcooked. Choose based on your preference for texture.
- **Customization:** Feel free to add other ingredients such as chopped bell peppers, radishes, or green onions for extra crunch and flavor.
- **Make Ahead:** Potato salad can be made a day in advance and stored in the refrigerator. Just give it a good stir before serving.

Enjoy your classic Potato Salad—a creamy, satisfying side dish that's always a crowd-pleaser!

Buffalo Chicken Wings

Ingredients:

For the Wings:

- **2 pounds chicken wings** (about 20-25 wings)
- **1 tablespoon baking powder** (not baking soda, for crispiness)
- **1/2 teaspoon salt**
- **1/2 teaspoon black pepper**

For the Buffalo Sauce:

- **1/2 cup hot sauce** (such as Frank's RedHot)
- **1/4 cup unsalted butter** (1/2 stick)
- **1 tablespoon white vinegar** (or apple cider vinegar)
- **1/2 teaspoon garlic powder**
- **1/2 teaspoon onion powder**
- **1/4 teaspoon cayenne pepper** (optional, for extra heat)

For Serving:

- **Celery sticks**
- **Carrot sticks**
- **Ranch or blue cheese dressing**

Instructions:

1. Prepare the Chicken Wings:

1. **Preheat Oven:** Preheat your oven to 400°F (200°C).
2. **Prep Wings:** If your chicken wings are whole, cut them into drumettes and flats. Discard the wing tips or save them for making broth.
3. **Dry Wings:** Pat the wings dry with paper towels. The drier they are, the crispier they will get.
4. **Coat with Baking Powder:** In a large bowl, toss the wings with baking powder, salt, and black pepper. The baking powder helps make the skin crispy.

2. Bake the Wings:

1. **Arrange on Rack:** Place a wire rack on a baking sheet and arrange the wings in a single layer on the rack. The rack allows air to circulate around the wings, helping them cook evenly and become crispy.
2. **Bake:** Bake in the preheated oven for 40-45 minutes, or until the wings are golden brown and crispy. Flip the wings halfway through for even cooking.

3. Make the Buffalo Sauce:

1. **Melt Butter:** While the wings are baking, melt the butter in a small saucepan over medium heat.

2. **Add Hot Sauce:** Stir in the hot sauce, vinegar, garlic powder, onion powder, and cayenne pepper (if using). Mix well and simmer for a few minutes, then remove from heat.

4. Toss the Wings:

   1. **Coat Wings:** Once the wings are done baking, transfer them to a large bowl. Pour the hot Buffalo sauce over the wings and toss until they are evenly coated.

5. Serve:

   1. **Serve with Sides:** Serve the Buffalo chicken wings hot with celery sticks, carrot sticks, and your choice of ranch or blue cheese dressing.

Tips:

- **Crispiness:** For extra crispy wings, make sure they are well-dried before coating with baking powder. You can also bake them on a convection setting if your oven has one.
- **Sauce:** Adjust the amount of hot sauce and cayenne pepper to suit your taste. If you prefer a milder sauce, reduce the hot sauce or add more butter.
- **Frying Option:** If you prefer frying over baking, heat oil in a deep fryer or large pot to 350°F (175°C) and fry the wings in batches until golden brown and crispy, about 8-10 minutes. Drain on paper towels and toss with sauce.

Enjoy your Buffalo Chicken Wings—a spicy, savory treat that's sure to be a hit at any gathering!

Tater Tot Casserole

Ingredients:

- **1 pound ground beef** (or ground turkey for a lighter option)
- **1 small onion**, chopped
- **2 cloves garlic**, minced
- **1 can (10.5 oz) cream of mushroom soup** (or cream of chicken soup)
- **1/2 cup milk**
- **1 cup frozen peas** (or mixed vegetables)
- **1 cup shredded cheddar cheese**
- **1 bag (32 oz) frozen tater tots**
- **Salt and black pepper** to taste
- **1 teaspoon dried thyme** (optional)
- **1 teaspoon dried parsley** (optional)

Instructions:

1. Preheat Oven:

1. **Preheat Oven:** Preheat your oven to 375°F (190°C).

2. Cook the Meat:

1. **Brown Beef:** In a large skillet over medium heat, cook the ground beef with the chopped onion and minced garlic until the meat is browned and the onion is translucent. Drain any excess fat.
2. **Season:** Season with salt, black pepper, and dried thyme (if using). Stir well.

3. Prepare the Sauce:

1. **Combine Soup and Milk:** In a bowl, mix together the cream of mushroom soup and milk until smooth.
2. **Add Vegetables:** Stir in the frozen peas (or mixed vegetables) and the cheese.

4. Assemble the Casserole:

1. **Mix Meat and Sauce:** Add the soup mixture to the cooked ground beef in the skillet. Stir well to combine.
2. **Transfer to Baking Dish:** Pour the meat and sauce mixture into a 9x13-inch baking dish or similar-sized casserole dish, spreading it evenly.
3. **Top with Tater Tots:** Arrange the frozen tater tots in a single layer on top of the meat mixture.

5. Bake the Casserole:

1. **Bake:** Place the casserole in the preheated oven and bake for 35-45 minutes, or until the tater tots are golden brown and crispy, and the casserole is bubbling around the edges.

6. Serve:

1. **Cool Slightly:** Allow the casserole to cool for a few minutes before serving. This helps it set and makes serving easier.

Tips:

- **Cheese Variations:** Feel free to use different types of cheese, such as mozzarella or a cheddar blend, for a different flavor.
- **Vegetables:** You can add other vegetables like corn, bell peppers, or mushrooms to the meat mixture if desired.
- **Meat Alternatives:** Ground turkey or chicken can be used instead of ground beef for a lighter version.

Enjoy your Tater Tot Casserole—a comforting and satisfying meal that's sure to be a hit with the whole family!

Beef and Noodle Casserole

Ingredients:

- **1 pound ground beef**
- **1 small onion**, chopped
- **2 cloves garlic**, minced
- **1 can (14.5 oz) diced tomatoes** (with or without green chilies)
- **1 can (10.5 oz) cream of mushroom soup** (or cream of chicken soup)
- **1 cup beef broth** (or chicken broth)
- **2 cups cooked egg noodles** (about 4 cups uncooked)
- **1 cup frozen peas** (or mixed vegetables)
- **1 cup shredded cheddar cheese** (or a cheese blend)
- **1 teaspoon dried Italian seasoning** (optional)
- **Salt and black pepper** to taste
- **1/2 cup grated Parmesan cheese** (optional, for topping)
- **1 tablespoon olive oil** (for cooking)

Instructions:

1. Preheat Oven:

1. **Preheat Oven:** Preheat your oven to 350°F (175°C).

2. Cook the Beef:

1. **Brown Beef:** In a large skillet, heat the olive oil over medium heat. Add the ground beef, chopped onion, and minced garlic. Cook until the beef is browned and the onion is translucent, breaking up the meat with a spoon as it cooks. Drain any excess fat.

3. Prepare the Sauce:

1. **Combine Ingredients:** Stir in the diced tomatoes, cream of mushroom soup, and beef broth. Mix well and simmer for a few minutes to blend the flavors. Season with salt, black pepper, and dried Italian seasoning (if using).

4. Combine Noodles and Vegetables:

1. **Mix Noodles:** In a large bowl, combine the cooked egg noodles, frozen peas (or mixed vegetables), and the beef mixture. Stir until everything is well combined.

5. Assemble the Casserole:

1. **Transfer to Baking Dish:** Pour the noodle and beef mixture into a greased 9x13-inch baking dish or similar-sized casserole dish.
2. **Add Cheese:** Sprinkle the shredded cheddar cheese evenly over the top of the casserole. If using, sprinkle with grated Parmesan cheese for extra flavor.

6. Bake:

1. **Bake:** Place the casserole in the preheated oven and bake for 25-30 minutes, or until the cheese is melted and bubbly, and the casserole is heated through.

7. Serve:

1. **Cool Slightly:** Allow the casserole to cool for a few minutes before serving. This helps it set and makes serving easier.

Tips:

- **Cheese Variations:** You can use different types of cheese based on your preference, such as mozzarella, gouda, or a cheese blend.
- **Vegetable Options:** Feel free to add other vegetables like mushrooms, bell peppers, or corn to the casserole.
- **Make Ahead:** This casserole can be assembled ahead of time and refrigerated until ready to bake. Just add a few extra minutes to the baking time if baking from cold.

Enjoy your Beef and Noodle Casserole—a warm, comforting dish that's sure to be a hit with the whole family!

Lemon Bars

Ingredients:

For the Crust:

- 1 1/2 cups all-purpose flour
- 1/2 cup granulated sugar
- 1/2 cup unsalted butter (1 stick, cold and cut into pieces)
- 1/4 teaspoon salt

For the Lemon Filling:

- 4 large eggs
- 1 1/2 cups granulated sugar
- 1/4 cup all-purpose flour
- 1/2 cup freshly squeezed lemon juice (about 2-3 lemons)
- 2 teaspoons lemon zest (optional, for extra lemon flavor)
- 1/2 teaspoon baking powder
- Powdered sugar (for dusting)

Instructions:

1. Preheat Oven:

1. **Preheat Oven:** Preheat your oven to 350°F (175°C). Grease and flour a 9x13-inch baking dish or line it with parchment paper.

2. Make the Crust:

1. **Combine Ingredients:** In a medium bowl, mix together the flour, granulated sugar, and salt.
2. **Cut in Butter:** Add the cold butter pieces to the flour mixture. Use a pastry cutter, fork, or your fingers to cut the butter into the flour until the mixture resembles coarse crumbs.
3. **Press into Pan:** Press the mixture evenly into the bottom of the prepared baking dish to form a crust.

3. Bake the Crust:

1. **Bake:** Bake the crust in the preheated oven for 15-20 minutes, or until it is lightly golden. Remove from the oven and set aside.

4. Prepare the Lemon Filling:

1. **Whisk Eggs:** In a large bowl, whisk the eggs until well beaten.
2. **Add Sugar and Flour:** Add the granulated sugar and flour to the eggs, and whisk until smooth.
3. **Mix in Lemon Juice:** Stir in the lemon juice and lemon zest (if using), and mix until well combined. Finally, add the baking powder and mix again.

5. Assemble and Bake:

1. **Pour Filling:** Pour the lemon filling over the pre-baked crust.
2. **Bake:** Return the dish to the oven and bake for an additional 25-30 minutes, or until the filling is set and no longer jiggles in the center. The top should be lightly golden and slightly cracked.

6. Cool and Serve:

1. **Cool:** Allow the lemon bars to cool completely in the pan on a wire rack. Once cooled, dust with powdered sugar.
2. **Cut into Bars:** Once completely cooled, cut into squares or bars.

Tips:

- **Lemon Juice:** For the best flavor, use freshly squeezed lemon juice. Bottled lemon juice can sometimes have a slightly different taste.
- **Crust:** For a thicker crust, use a smaller baking dish, or increase the crust ingredients proportionally.
- **Storage:** Lemon bars can be stored in an airtight container at room temperature for up to 3 days, or refrigerated for up to a week. They also freeze well for up to 3 months.

Enjoy your Lemon Bars—a delightful balance of sweet and tart with a buttery crust that makes for a refreshing and satisfying treat!

Peach Cobbler

Ingredients:

For the Peach Filling:

- **6 cups fresh peaches** (peeled, pitted, and sliced, or about 4 cups canned peaches, drained)
- **1 cup granulated sugar**
- **2 tablespoons cornstarch**
- **1 teaspoon ground cinnamon**
- **1/4 teaspoon ground nutmeg**
- **1 tablespoon lemon juice** (or 1 teaspoon lemon zest)
- **1/4 teaspoon salt**

For the Cobbler Topping:

- **1 cup all-purpose flour**
- **1/2 cup granulated sugar**
- **1/2 cup packed brown sugar**
- **1 1/2 teaspoons baking powder**
- **1/2 teaspoon salt**
- **1/2 cup unsalted butter** (1 stick, cold and cut into pieces)
- **1/2 cup milk** (whole milk or buttermilk works best)
- **1 teaspoon vanilla extract**

Optional for Serving:

- **Vanilla ice cream** or **whipped cream**

Instructions:

1. Preheat Oven:

1. **Preheat Oven:** Preheat your oven to 375°F (190°C).

2. Prepare the Peach Filling:

1. **Mix Ingredients:** In a large bowl, combine the peaches, granulated sugar, cornstarch, ground cinnamon, ground nutmeg, lemon juice, and salt. Stir well to coat the peaches evenly.
2. **Transfer to Dish:** Pour the peach mixture into a greased 9x13-inch baking dish or a similar-sized oven-safe dish.

3. Make the Cobbler Topping:

1. **Combine Dry Ingredients:** In a medium bowl, mix together the flour, granulated sugar, brown sugar, baking powder, and salt.
2. **Cut in Butter:** Add the cold butter pieces to the dry ingredients. Use a pastry cutter, fork, or your fingers to cut the butter into the mixture until it resembles coarse crumbs.

3. **Add Liquid Ingredients:** Stir in the milk and vanilla extract until just combined. The batter will be thick.

4. Assemble the Cobbler:

1. **Drop Topping:** Spoon dollops of the cobbler topping over the peach filling. It doesn't need to cover the peaches completely; some gaps are fine. The topping will spread out as it bakes.

5. Bake:

1. **Bake:** Bake in the preheated oven for 45-50 minutes, or until the topping is golden brown and a toothpick inserted into the topping comes out clean. The peach filling should be bubbling around the edges.

6. Serve:

1. **Cool Slightly:** Allow the cobbler to cool for a few minutes before serving. This helps the filling to set slightly.
2. **Serve:** Serve warm, optionally with a scoop of vanilla ice cream or a dollop of whipped cream.

Tips:

- **Peach Preparation:** If using fresh peaches, blanch them in boiling water for 30 seconds to make peeling easier. You can also use frozen peaches, but make sure they are thawed and drained before using.
- **Topping Variation:** For a slightly different topping, you can use biscuit mix or a cake mix for a quicker version.
- **Storage:** Peach cobbler can be stored in an airtight container at room temperature for up to 2 days, or refrigerated for up to 5 days. It can also be frozen for up to 3 months. Reheat in the oven for the best texture.

Enjoy your Peach Cobbler—a delightful, warm dessert that combines the sweetness of peaches with a perfectly baked topping!

Apple Pie

Ingredients:

For the Pie Crust:

- **2 1/2 cups all-purpose flour**
- **1 teaspoon granulated sugar**
- **1 teaspoon salt**
- **1 cup (2 sticks) unsalted butter**, cold and cut into small pieces
- **6-8 tablespoons ice water**

For the Apple Filling:

- **6-7 cups apples** (about 6-8 medium apples, preferably a mix of tart and sweet like Granny Smith and Honeycrisp)
- **3/4 cup granulated sugar**
- **1/4 cup packed brown sugar**
- **1/4 cup all-purpose flour** (or cornstarch)
- **1 teaspoon ground cinnamon**
- **1/4 teaspoon ground nutmeg**
- **1/4 teaspoon ground allspice** (optional)
- **1 tablespoon lemon juice** (or 1 teaspoon lemon zest)
- **1/2 teaspoon vanilla extract** (optional)
- **Pinch of salt**

For Assembling:

- **1 large egg**, beaten (for egg wash)
- **1 tablespoon granulated sugar** (for sprinkling on top)

Instructions:

1. Make the Pie Crust:

1. **Mix Dry Ingredients:** In a large bowl, combine the flour, granulated sugar, and salt.
2. **Cut in Butter:** Add the cold butter pieces. Use a pastry cutter, fork, or your fingers to cut the butter into the flour mixture until it resembles coarse crumbs with pea-sized pieces of butter remaining.
3. **Add Ice Water:** Gradually add ice water, one tablespoon at a time, mixing just until the dough comes together. You may not need all the water.
4. **Chill Dough:** Divide the dough in half, shape each half into a disc, wrap in plastic wrap, and refrigerate for at least 1 hour.

2. Prepare the Apple Filling:

1. **Peel and Slice Apples:** Peel, core, and slice the apples into thin, even slices.
2. **Mix Filling:** In a large bowl, toss the apple slices with granulated sugar, brown sugar, flour (or cornstarch), cinnamon, nutmeg, allspice (if using), lemon juice, and vanilla extract until well coated. Set aside.

3. Assemble the Pie:

1. **Preheat Oven:** Preheat your oven to 425°F (220°C).
2. **Roll Out Dough:** On a lightly floured surface, roll out one disc of dough to fit a 9-inch pie dish. Carefully transfer the dough to the dish and trim any excess hanging over the edges.
3. **Add Filling:** Spoon the apple filling into the prepared pie crust, mounding slightly in the center.
4. **Top Crust:** Roll out the second disc of dough and place it over the filling. Trim, fold, and crimp the edges to seal. Cut a few slits in the top crust to allow steam to escape. Alternatively, you can make a lattice crust.
5. **Apply Egg Wash:** Brush the top crust with the beaten egg and sprinkle with granulated sugar.

4. Bake the Pie:

1. **Bake:** Bake in the preheated oven for 45-55 minutes, or until the crust is golden brown and the filling is bubbling. If the crust begins to brown too quickly, cover the edges with foil.
2. **Cool:** Allow the pie to cool on a wire rack for at least 2 hours before serving. This helps the filling to set and makes slicing easier.

Tips:

- **Apple Variety:** A mix of apples provides a balance of tartness and sweetness. Granny Smiths are tart and hold their shape well, while Honeycrisps or Fujis add sweetness.
- **Crust Handling:** If the dough is too soft to work with, chill it again for a few minutes. If it cracks or tears, you can patch it with extra dough.
- **Thickening Filling:** If the filling seems too runny, you can use additional flour or cornstarch to thicken it. Add a bit more if necessary before assembling the pie.

Enjoy your Apple Pie— a timeless classic that's sure to delight with its buttery crust and flavorful apple filling!

Bread Pudding

Ingredients:

For the Bread Pudding:

- **6 cups stale bread cubes** (about 1 loaf, preferably French or Italian bread)
- **4 large eggs**
- **2 1/2 cups whole milk** (or any milk you prefer)
- **1 cup granulated sugar**
- **1/2 cup packed brown sugar**
- **1/2 cup raisins** (or other dried fruit, optional)
- **1 teaspoon vanilla extract**
- **1 teaspoon ground cinnamon**
- **1/2 teaspoon ground nutmeg**
- **1/4 teaspoon salt**
- **1/4 cup unsalted butter** (melted, for greasing the pan and adding richness)

For the Sauce (Optional):

- **1/2 cup heavy cream**
- **1/4 cup granulated sugar**
- **2 tablespoons unsalted butter**
- **1 teaspoon vanilla extract**
- **1 tablespoon bourbon or rum** (optional, for flavor)

Instructions:

1. Prepare the Bread Pudding:

1. **Preheat Oven:** Preheat your oven to 350°F (175°C). Grease a 9x13-inch baking dish or similar-sized dish with butter.
2. **Prepare Bread:** If the bread isn't already stale, toast the cubes lightly in the oven for a few minutes until they are dry. Place the bread cubes in a large bowl.
3. **Mix Wet Ingredients:** In a separate bowl, whisk together the eggs, milk, granulated sugar, brown sugar, vanilla extract, ground cinnamon, ground nutmeg, and salt until well combined.
4. **Combine:** Pour the egg mixture over the bread cubes and stir gently to coat the bread. Let it sit for 10-15 minutes to allow the bread to absorb the liquid. Gently fold in the raisins if using.

2. Bake the Bread Pudding:

1. **Transfer to Dish:** Pour the bread mixture into the prepared baking dish, spreading it evenly.
2. **Bake:** Bake in the preheated oven for 45-55 minutes, or until the pudding is set and the top is golden brown. A knife inserted into the center should come out clean. The pudding should be slightly puffed and firm to the touch.

3. Prepare the Sauce (Optional):

1. **Combine Ingredients:** In a small saucepan over medium heat, combine the heavy cream, granulated sugar, and butter. Stir until the butter and sugar are melted and the mixture is smooth.
2. **Simmer:** Bring the mixture to a simmer and cook for a few minutes until slightly thickened. Remove from heat and stir in the vanilla extract and bourbon or rum if using.

4. Serve:

1. **Cool Slightly:** Allow the bread pudding to cool for a few minutes before serving. It can be served warm or at room temperature.
2. **Top with Sauce:** Serve with a drizzle of the prepared sauce, or with a scoop of vanilla ice cream or whipped cream.

Tips:

- **Bread:** Use slightly stale or toasted bread for the best texture. Fresh bread can become too mushy.
- **Variations:** You can add other mix-ins like nuts (pecans or walnuts), chocolate chips, or fresh fruit (like apples or berries).
- **Make Ahead:** Bread pudding can be assembled a day in advance and baked before serving. Just cover and refrigerate the unbaked pudding, then bake as directed.

Enjoy your Bread Pudding—a delicious and comforting dessert that's perfect for cozy gatherings and a great way to use up leftover bread!

Chocolate Cake

Ingredients:

For the Cake:

- 1 3/4 cups all-purpose flour
- 1 1/2 cups granulated sugar
- 3/4 cup unsweetened cocoa powder (preferably Dutch-processed)
- 1 1/2 teaspoons baking powder
- 1 1/2 teaspoons baking soda
- 1 teaspoon salt
- 2 large eggs
- 1 cup whole milk (or any milk you prefer)
- 1/2 cup vegetable oil
- 2 teaspoons vanilla extract
- 1 cup boiling water

For the Chocolate Frosting:

- 1/2 cup (1 stick) unsalted butter, softened
- 2/3 cup unsweetened cocoa powder
- 3 cups powdered sugar
- 1/3 cup whole milk (or more if needed)
- 1 teaspoon vanilla extract
- Pinch of salt

Instructions:

1. Prepare the Cake Batter:

1. **Preheat Oven:** Preheat your oven to 350°F (175°C). Grease and flour two 9-inch round cake pans or line them with parchment paper.
2. **Mix Dry Ingredients:** In a large bowl, sift together the flour, granulated sugar, cocoa powder, baking powder, baking soda, and salt.
3. **Combine Wet Ingredients:** In another bowl, whisk together the eggs, milk, vegetable oil, and vanilla extract until well combined.
4. **Mix Batter:** Gradually add the wet ingredients to the dry ingredients, mixing until smooth. Stir in the boiling water until the batter is well combined. The batter will be thin.
5. **Pour and Bake:** Divide the batter evenly between the prepared cake pans. Bake for 30-35 minutes, or until a toothpick inserted into the center comes out clean.

2. Cool the Cakes:

1. **Cool:** Allow the cakes to cool in the pans for about 10 minutes, then transfer them to a wire rack to cool completely before frosting.

3. Prepare the Chocolate Frosting:

1. **Beat Butter:** In a medium bowl, beat the softened butter with an electric mixer until creamy.
2. **Add Cocoa Powder:** Gradually add the cocoa powder and beat until combined.

3. **Add Sugar and Milk:** Add the powdered sugar and milk alternately, starting and ending with powdered sugar, until the frosting reaches your desired consistency. Beat in the vanilla extract and a pinch of salt.
4. **Adjust Consistency:** If the frosting is too thick, add a little more milk. If it's too thin, add more powdered sugar.

4. Frost the Cake:

1. **Assemble Cake:** Place one cake layer on a serving plate or cake stand. Spread a layer of frosting on top. Place the second cake layer on top of the frosting.
2. **Frost the Cake:** Spread the remaining frosting evenly over the top and sides of the cake.

Tips:

- **Cake Layers:** Ensure the cakes are completely cooled before frosting to prevent the frosting from melting.
- **Frosting Consistency:** Adjust the frosting consistency as needed. It should be spreadable but not too runny.
- **Decorations:** For added decoration, you can garnish with chocolate shavings, sprinkles, or fresh berries.

Enjoy your Classic Chocolate Cake—a rich and decadent treat that's perfect for any chocolate lover!

Banana Pudding

Ingredients:

For the Pudding:

- 1/2 cup granulated sugar
- 1/3 cup all-purpose flour
- 1/4 teaspoon salt
- 2 3/4 cups whole milk
- 3 large egg yolks
- 2 tablespoons unsalted butter
- 1 teaspoon vanilla extract

For the Assembly:

- **4-5 ripe bananas**, sliced
- **1 box (12 oz) vanilla wafers** (or other similar cookies)
- **Whipped cream** (optional, for topping)

Instructions:

1. Prepare the Pudding:

1. **Mix Dry Ingredients:** In a medium saucepan, whisk together the granulated sugar, flour, and salt.
2. **Add Milk:** Gradually add the milk to the dry ingredients, whisking continuously to combine.
3. **Cook Pudding:** Cook the mixture over medium heat, stirring constantly, until it starts to thicken and bubble. This usually takes about 8-10 minutes.
4. **Temper the Egg Yolks:** While the mixture is heating, lightly beat the egg yolks in a small bowl. Once the milk mixture is hot, gradually add a small amount of the hot mixture to the egg yolks to temper them. Then, whisk the tempered egg yolks back into the saucepan.
5. **Finish Cooking:** Continue cooking the mixture for another 2-3 minutes, stirring constantly until it thickens further.
6. **Remove from Heat:** Remove the saucepan from heat and stir in the butter and vanilla extract. Mix until the butter is melted and the pudding is smooth.

2. Assemble the Banana Pudding:

1. **Layer Pudding:** In a large serving dish or individual cups, start by layering vanilla wafers on the bottom.
2. **Add Bananas:** Place a layer of banana slices over the wafers.
3. **Add Pudding:** Spoon a layer of pudding over the bananas and wafers.
4. **Repeat Layers:** Repeat the layers until all the ingredients are used, finishing with a layer of pudding on top.
5. **Chill:** Cover and refrigerate the banana pudding for at least 4 hours, or overnight, to allow the flavors to meld and the wafers to soften.

3. Serve:

1. **Top with Whipped Cream:** Just before serving, you can top the pudding with whipped cream if desired. You can also garnish with additional banana slices or crushed vanilla wafers.

Tips:

- **Bananas:** To prevent the bananas from browning, add them to the pudding just before serving or toss them with a little lemon juice before layering.
- **Pudding Consistency:** If the pudding seems too thick after chilling, you can gently stir in a little milk to reach your desired consistency.
- **Variations:** For a different twist, you can add a layer of caramel sauce or chocolate pudding.

Enjoy your Classic Banana Pudding—a delightful, creamy dessert that's sure to be a hit with family and friends!

Key Lime Pie

Ingredients:

For the Graham Cracker Crust:

- **1 1/2 cups graham cracker crumbs** (about 10-12 graham crackers)

- **1/4 cup granulated sugar**
- **1/2 cup unsalted butter** (1 stick, melted)

For the Key Lime Filling:

- **1 can (14 oz) sweetened condensed milk**
- **1/2 cup sour cream**
- **1/2 cup freshly squeezed key lime juice** (about 10-12 key limes, or regular lime juice can be used)
- **3 large egg yolks**

For the Topping (Optional):

- **1 cup heavy cream**
- **2 tablespoons granulated sugar**
- **1 teaspoon vanilla extract**
- **Lime zest** (for garnish)

Instructions:

1. Prepare the Graham Cracker Crust:

1. **Preheat Oven:** Preheat your oven to 350°F (175°C).
2. **Mix Crust Ingredients:** In a medium bowl, combine the graham cracker crumbs, granulated sugar, and melted butter. Mix until the crumbs are well coated and the mixture resembles wet sand.
3. **Press into Pan:** Press the crumb mixture evenly into the bottom and up the sides of a 9-inch pie pan. Use the back of a spoon or a flat-bottomed glass to press the crumbs firmly.
4. **Bake:** Bake the crust in the preheated oven for 8-10 minutes, or until lightly golden. Remove from the oven and let it cool while you prepare the filling.

2. Prepare the Key Lime Filling:

1. **Mix Filling Ingredients:** In a large bowl, whisk together the sweetened condensed milk, sour cream, key lime juice, and egg yolks until smooth and well combined.
2. **Pour Filling:** Pour the filling into the cooled graham cracker crust.

3. Bake the Pie:

1. **Bake:** Bake in the preheated oven for 15-18 minutes, or until the filling is set and slightly puffed. The edges should look set, but the center might still jiggle a bit.
2. **Cool:** Allow the pie to cool to room temperature, then refrigerate for at least 3 hours, or overnight, to fully set and chill.

4. Prepare the Topping (Optional):

1. **Whip Cream:** In a large bowl, beat the heavy cream, granulated sugar, and vanilla extract with an electric mixer until stiff peaks form.
2. **Top Pie:** Spread or pipe the whipped cream over the chilled pie.
3. **Garnish:** Garnish with lime zest if desired.

Tips:

- **Key Limes:** Key limes are smaller and more tart than regular limes, but if you can't find them, regular lime juice is a good substitute.
- **Whipped Cream:** For a firmer topping, make sure the cream and bowl are well-chilled before whipping.
- **Pie Shell:** Ensure the crust is completely cooled before adding the filling to prevent it from becoming soggy.

Enjoy your Classic Key Lime Pie—a refreshing and tangy dessert that's perfect for warm weather or any time you want a taste of the tropics!

Pecan Pie

Ingredients:

For the Pie Crust:

- **1 1/4 cups all-purpose flour**
- **1/4 teaspoon salt**
- **1/4 cup granulated sugar**
- **1/2 cup (1 stick) unsalted butter**, cold and cut into small pieces
- **1/4 cup ice water** (more if needed)

For the Pecan Filling:

- **1 cup light corn syrup**
- **1 cup granulated sugar**
- **1/4 cup unsalted butter**, melted
- **3 large eggs**
- **1 1/2 teaspoons vanilla extract**
- **1/2 teaspoon salt**
- **1 1/2 cups pecan halves** (about 6 oz)

Instructions:

1. Prepare the Pie Crust:

1. **Mix Dry Ingredients:** In a large bowl, whisk together the flour, salt, and granulated sugar.
2. **Cut in Butter:** Add the cold butter pieces to the flour mixture. Use a pastry cutter, fork, or your fingers to cut the butter into the flour until the mixture resembles coarse crumbs.
3. **Add Ice Water:** Gradually add the ice water, one tablespoon at a time, mixing just until the dough comes together. It should be moist but not sticky.
4. **Chill Dough:** Shape the dough into a disk, wrap it in plastic wrap, and refrigerate for at least 1 hour.

2. Prepare the Pie Crust for Baking:

1. **Preheat Oven:** Preheat your oven to 375°F (190°C).
2. **Roll Out Dough:** On a lightly floured surface, roll out the dough to fit a 9-inch pie dish. Carefully transfer the dough to the pie dish and trim any excess. Crimp the edges as desired.
3. **Blind Bake (Optional):** For a crisper crust, you can blind bake the crust. To do this, line the crust with parchment paper and fill it with pie weights or dried beans. Bake for 10-12 minutes, then remove the weights and parchment and bake for an additional 5 minutes. Let cool slightly before adding the filling.

3. Prepare the Pecan Filling:

1. **Mix Ingredients:** In a large bowl, whisk together the corn syrup, granulated sugar, melted butter, eggs, vanilla extract, and salt until well combined.
2. **Add Pecans:** Stir in the pecan halves.

4. Assemble and Bake the Pie:

1. **Pour Filling:** Pour the pecan filling into the prepared pie crust.
2. **Bake:** Bake in the preheated oven for 50-60 minutes, or until the filling is set and the top is golden brown. The center should be slightly jiggly but should set up as it cools. If the crust begins to brown too quickly, cover the edges with aluminum foil.
3. **Cool:** Allow the pie to cool completely on a wire rack before serving. This allows the filling to fully set.

Tips:

- **Corn Syrup:** Light corn syrup is typically used for a classic pecan pie. Dark corn syrup can be used for a richer flavor, but it will darken the filling.
- **Pecans:** Toasting the pecans lightly before adding them to the filling can enhance their flavor.
- **Storage:** Pecan pie can be stored at room temperature for up to 3 days or in the refrigerator for up to a week. It can also be frozen for up to 3 months. Reheat in a 300°F (150°C) oven to serve warm.

Enjoy your Classic Pecan Pie—a sweet, nutty treat that's sure to be a hit at any gathering!

Rice Pudding

Ingredients:

- **1/2 cup short-grain or medium-grain rice** (such as Arborio or sushi rice)
- **1 1/2 cups water**

- **2 cups whole milk**
- **1/2 cup granulated sugar**
- **1/4 teaspoon salt**
- **1/2 teaspoon vanilla extract**
- **1/4 teaspoon ground cinnamon** (optional)
- **1/4 cup raisins** (optional)
- **1 tablespoon unsalted butter** (optional, for extra creaminess)

Instructions:

1. Cook the Rice:

1. **Rinse Rice:** Rinse the rice under cold water until the water runs clear to remove excess starch.
2. **Cook Rice:** In a medium saucepan, combine the rice and water. Bring to a boil over medium-high heat. Reduce the heat to low, cover, and simmer for about 15-20 minutes, or until the water is absorbed and the rice is tender.

2. Prepare the Pudding:

1. **Combine Ingredients:** In a separate large saucepan, combine the cooked rice, milk, sugar, and salt.
2. **Cook Pudding:** Bring the mixture to a simmer over medium heat, stirring frequently. Reduce the heat to low and continue to cook, stirring occasionally, until the mixture thickens and becomes creamy. This usually takes about 20-25 minutes.
3. **Add Flavorings:** Stir in the vanilla extract and ground cinnamon if using. You can also add raisins at this point if desired. For extra creaminess, stir in the butter.

3. Serve:

1. **Cool:** Allow the rice pudding to cool slightly before serving. It can be enjoyed warm or chilled.
2. **Garnish:** Serve with additional ground cinnamon on top if desired. You can also garnish with fresh fruit or a drizzle of honey.

Tips:

- **Rice Texture:** For a creamier texture, use short-grain or medium-grain rice. Long-grain rice doesn't release as much starch, so it will result in a less creamy pudding.
- **Adjust Sweetness:** Taste the pudding before serving and adjust the sweetness if needed by adding a little more sugar.
- **Flavor Variations:** For a different flavor, you can add a pinch of nutmeg, a splash of almond extract, or a handful of chopped nuts.

Enjoy your Classic Rice Pudding—a delightful, creamy dessert that's both comforting and versatile!

Caramel Apple Cake

Ingredients:

For the Cake:

- 1 1/2 cups all-purpose flour
- 1 teaspoon baking powder

- 1/2 teaspoon baking soda
- 1/2 teaspoon salt
- 1/2 teaspoon ground cinnamon
- 1/4 teaspoon ground nutmeg
- **1/2 cup unsalted butter** (1 stick), softened
- **1 cup granulated sugar**
- **2 large eggs**
- **1 teaspoon vanilla extract**
- **1/2 cup sour cream** (or plain yogurt)
- **1 cup peeled and diced apples** (about 1-2 apples, such as Granny Smith or Honeycrisp)
- **1/4 cup chopped nuts** (optional, such as walnuts or pecans)

For the Caramel Sauce:

- **1 cup granulated sugar**
- **6 tablespoons unsalted butter** (cut into pieces)
- **1/4 cup heavy cream**
- **1/2 teaspoon vanilla extract**
- **Pinch of salt**

Instructions:

1. Prepare the Cake:

1. **Preheat Oven:** Preheat your oven to 350°F (175°C). Grease and flour a 9-inch round cake pan or line it with parchment paper.
2. **Mix Dry Ingredients:** In a medium bowl, whisk together the flour, baking powder, baking soda, salt, cinnamon, and nutmeg.
3. **Cream Butter and Sugar:** In a large bowl, beat the softened butter and granulated sugar together until light and fluffy.
4. **Add Eggs and Vanilla:** Add the eggs one at a time, beating well after each addition. Mix in the vanilla extract.
5. **Add Dry Ingredients and Sour Cream:** Gradually add the dry ingredients to the butter mixture, alternating with the sour cream, beginning and ending with the dry ingredients. Mix until just combined.
6. **Fold in Apples and Nuts:** Gently fold in the diced apples and chopped nuts if using.
7. **Bake Cake:** Pour the batter into the prepared cake pan and smooth the top. Bake for 30-35 minutes, or until a toothpick inserted into the center comes out clean.
8. **Cool Cake:** Allow the cake to cool in the pan for 10 minutes before transferring it to a wire rack to cool completely.

2. Prepare the Caramel Sauce:

1. **Melt Sugar:** In a medium saucepan over medium heat, melt the granulated sugar, stirring constantly. It will first turn into a liquid and then begin to brown.
2. **Add Butter:** Once the sugar is fully melted and amber-colored, carefully add the butter pieces. Stir until the butter is fully melted and combined.
3. **Add Cream and Vanilla:** Slowly pour in the heavy cream, stirring constantly. Be careful as the mixture may bubble up. Stir until smooth and combined.
4. **Add Salt:** Stir in the vanilla extract and a pinch of salt. Remove from heat and let the sauce cool slightly.

3. Serve:

1. **Top Cake:** Once the cake is completely cooled, drizzle the caramel sauce over the top.
2. **Garnish (Optional):** Garnish with extra chopped nuts or a sprinkle of sea salt if desired.

Tips:

- **Apples:** Use firm apples that hold their shape well during baking.
- **Caramel Sauce:** The caramel sauce can be made ahead of time and stored in the refrigerator. Reheat gently before using.
- **Texture:** If the cake is too dense or heavy, it might be due to overmixing. Mix until just combined to keep the cake light and tender.

Enjoy your Caramel Apple Cake—a perfect blend of sweet, fruity, and caramel flavors in every bite!

www.ingramcontent.com/pod-product-compliance
Lightning Source LLC
LaVergne TN
LVHW081557060526
838201LV00054B/1937